BEYOND SIBLING RIVALRY

BEYOND
SIBLING
RIVALRY

How to Help Your Children

Become Cooperative, Caring, and

Compassionate

Peter Goldenthal, Ph.D.

HENRY HOLT AND COMPANY
NEW YORK

S

Henry Holt and Company, Inc.
Publishers since 1866
115 West 18th Street
New York, New York 10011

Henry Holt® is a registered
trademark of Henry Holt and Company, Inc.

Library of Congress Cataloging-in-Publication Data
Goldenthal, Peter, date.
Beyond sibling rivalry: how to help your children become cooperative, caring,
and compassionate / Peter Goldenthal.—1st ed.
p.   cm.
Includes bibliographical references and index.
ISBN 0-8050-5688-2 (hardcover: alk. paper)
1. Sibling rivalry.   2. Sibling rivalry—Case studies.   3. Parent and child.
4. Family.   5. Child rearing.   I. Title.
BF723.S43G65   1999   98-21712
649'.1—dc21   CIP

Henry Holt books are available for special promotions and
premiums. For details contact: Director, Special Markets.

First Edition 1999

Designed by Kate Nichols

Printed in the United States of America
All first editions are printed on acid-free paper. ∞

10   9   8   7   6   5   4   3   2   1

For Wendy

CONTENTS

Contents

ACKNOWLEDGMENTS

First of all I wish to acknowledge my very great debt to Professor Ivan Boszormenyi-Nagy who has been teacher, mentor, confidant, and friend for the past fifteen years. I have had many rich discussions and exchanges of ideas with my colleagues in psychology and developmental and behavioral pediatrics at Children's Seashore House, in Philadelphia, especially Drs. Nathan Blum, William Carey, John Parrish, and Mary Pipan. Susan Munro's enthusiasm and encouragement were invaluable as I began writing this book. Roberta Israeloff provided advice and counsel based on her years as a writer that helped me tremendously at several crucial points. Lynn Seligman believed in this project from the beginning and helped me in many ways to realize it fully, most of all by finding it a home at Henry Holt. Cynthia Vartan, my editor at Henry Holt, has been a writer's dream: blending support, encouragement, wise counsel, pointed criticism, and reassurance in just the right proportions. These acknowledgments would not be complete without recognition of the support and love I have received from my wife, Wendy; children, Ariel, Mathew, Rebecca, and Sara; father, Carol Goldenthal; mother, Jolene Bleich Goldenthal; brother, Lance; and sister-in-law, Jann.

BEYOND SIBLING RIVALRY

INTRODUCTION

I t's *my* doll!" five-year-old Lucretia screams as she yanks her old and tattered Raggedy Ann from the arms of her two-year-old sister, Natasha, leaving Natasha wailing as she falls backward, hitting her head on the floor. It is only nine-thirty on that Tuesday morning, but it feels like midnight to Sally Jamison, Lucretia and Natasha's mother.

Sally arrived at motherhood as well prepared as anyone could be. She was an avid baby-sitter and camp counselor during high school. She majored in child development in college, taught in a nursery school for two years after graduation, and had seriously thought about starting her own day care center. She reads all the most highly recommended parenting books and loves her children. But when a morning starts to go this way, Sally begins to imagine taking a long vacation very far away—alone. It is not just the fighting that bothers her. She loves both her children so much, it hurts her that they are at each other's throats from the moment they awaken. She feels that down deep they love each other, too: she just wishes they would show it instead of fighting all the time. Her fondest hope is that they will be friends, now and throughout their lives.

In the twenty years that I have been working with children and their families, I have met many children like Lucretia and Natasha and many parents like Sally Jamison. Parents do worry about their children's fighting and wonder how they will ever learn to get along. Some parents hope that their children will grow out of their conflicts; others resign themselves to it, believing that conflicts among children reflect natural jealousies and that all firstborn children naturally wish they were still the only children in their families. But sibling relationships are much more than either biologically predetermined results of birth order or mere jealousies or fantasies about being an only child. To understand and improve relationships among children in a family, we must think about the web of family relationships, including relationships between parents and their parents, as important contexts in which sibling relationships develop. Sibling relationships are especially important because they set the stage for other close relationships: a child who has learned to appreciate a brother's or sister's point of view, to be sensitive to a brother's or sister's feelings, to enjoy closeness, to be able to stand up for his rights, and to enjoy the feeling of giving to another person has a big advantage in developing other close relationships, including friendships in older childhood and in adulthood.

The person who has done more than any other to advance my understanding of family relationships is the Hungarian-born psychiatrist Ivan Boszormenyi-Nagy. His *contextual theory* has been hugely influential for over three decades among psychologists, psychiatrists, social workers, and others whose professional work centers on helping families improve the way they talk to each other, live together, and share important moments together. The contextual perspective focus is both broader (considering the entire family as the context for sibling relationships) and deeper (attending to issues of fairness and justice among family members) than other, earlier ways of looking at family life.

I first met Ivan Boszormenyi-Nagy in 1984 and began to apply contextual ideas in my work shortly thereafter. Since then I have repeatedly been impressed by the power of this way of thinking about relationships to help all kinds of people in all sorts of quandaries. I have been especially impressed by the way that contextual ideas and techniques help parents teach their children how to get along with each other, how to be cooperative, and how to take pleasure from being caring and giving rather than fiercely competitive and angry.

Conflicted relationships among children in a family are troubling for everyone. Children are always upset by them, often far more than they appear to be, and almost always carry these feelings into other relationships at home and at school. Children who have very conflicted relationships with a brother or sister carry scars from those early hurts forever, and the scars affect not only their future relationships with that brother or sister, but relationships with other adults and often with their own children.

Beyond Sibling Rivalry introduces a new way of thinking about family relationships of all kinds that will help you see your children's relationships with each other in the context of the family as a whole and help you prevent many instances of sibling conflict and unnecessary jealousies, especially among very young children. I provide you with specific and practical strategies, techniques, and guidelines for preventing and reducing friction, stress, and conflict among your children. These include recognizing how unfairness leads to anger and sibling conflicts, giving each child credit for efforts and accomplishments, and being alert to the risk of letting your own childhood experiences interfere with your ability to see your children's hopes, needs, and concerns clearly. I also cover common and not-so-common sibling conflicts such as those involving sharing toys or friends, physical aggression between young children, and conflicts among stepsiblings. You will learn that bribery can be a positive and helpful technique, that acknowledgment of even small cooperative moments will enhance self-esteem *and* lead to more cooperation, and that *you* can greatly influence how your children respond to each other by changing how you respond to them. I show you how to apply these techniques in dealing with a great number of different problem situations, including difficulties with peers and at school.

Beyond Sibling Rivalry's greatest value, however, will be if it helps you to help your children become the sort of self-confident, sensitive, considerate, cooperative, compassionate, and caring children who enjoy being able to help each other, who get more satisfaction out of knowing that they have done something to contribute to the family and to their brother or sister than they do from one-upping them.

As you read *Beyond Sibling Rivalry* you will encounter many illustrations drawn from my professional work with children and families as well as from the questions and comments of parents who have attended my workshops, lectures, and informal talks. Although I have carefully disguised each family's stories by changing names and other identifying information, the situations and concerns are true.

As you read this book you will learn

- that how your children get along is influenced by how you and your parents got along when you were a child and by how you and your siblings got along as well.
- to recognize and highlight each child's unique abilities and interests.
- to recognize and acknowledge your children's imperfect efforts to be helpful to each other.
- to consider the possibility that you may inadvertently be replicating your own childhood conflicts in your children.
- to understand how children's loyalties may put them in terrible binds.
- to teach your children to be empathic.
- to help children learn to be assertive so they will not need to be aggressive.
- to sort out the differences between your issues and concerns and those of your children.

CHAPTER 1

Predictable and Preventable Sibling Conflicts

Julia and Frank said nothing to two-and-a-half-year-old Andy about the anticipated arrival of the new baby until they started disassembling his crib about two weeks before the baby's due date. When Andy asked where his bed was going, they told him it was for the new baby and that he would be sleeping in a "big boy bed." When Julia went to the hospital to give birth to Melissa, Andy went to stay with his grandmother. Julia's labor was longer than she expected, and she was very tired, so her mother offered to take care of Andy until she had gotten some rest: Andy stayed with her for three weeks. When he asked, "Where is my mommy?" his grandmother told him that his mother was with the new baby and that he would be home with her soon. When Julia and Frank picked him up they were surprised and distressed that he was sucking his thumb, something he had not done for a year. They were also surprised that he did not seem to be interested in his little sister at all, and they were shocked and frightened when, two months or eleven and calls for just as much thoughtful action from parents, perhaps even more. Melissa's parents divorced when she was five. Melissa's mother remarried five years later and became pregnant almost immediately. In preparation for the arrival of the new baby, Melissa's mother and stepfather hired a contractor to put an addition on their house consisting of a master bedroom suite and adjacent nursery. They lavished much care and attention on the design of the nursery, making sure that it had many sunny windows, pleasant views of the garden with its roses and bird feeders, and of course engaging and child-pleasing wallpaper and carpets. For all the thought they put into preparing for their new arrival, they forgot about Melissa, whose small third-floor room had seemed wonderfully private and special even if it was tiny and old-fashioned looking but now seemed so dingy and second-rate, in need of a coat of paint or some new wallpaper, in comparison with the new parts of the house. Unfortunately they did not learn how hurt Melissa had felt to see all this attention paid to the baby's room until years later, when they were troubled by the surprisingly strong resentment Melissa felt toward her little sister.

Do not worry that too much talk about the new baby will make your older child jealous. The important issue is not whether or not you talk about the new baby, but what you say about the baby, and especially what you say about your older child or children. The prospect of becoming a big brother or big sister is very exciting for a child of any age. The more you emphasize the role that your older child will play, the more you acknowledge how important he or she will be to the new baby, the less you will have to worry about jealousy. And be cautious about accepting offers from well-meaning relatives to have your older child visit them for extended periods of time after the baby's birth. It is best not to accept these generous invitations. If relatives wish to help when your new baby arrives, invite them to stay with you rather than send your older child off with them. Like Ted and Emily, you will have done much to start your children off in the right direction toward developing a happy, cooperative relationship that can be a model for other relationships later in life.

When parents ask what they can do to prevent sibling rivalry, some people may feel that the question is naive, that sibling rivalry is inevitable and cannot be prevented. It is true that children will always experience conflicts, and even moments of jealousy, but the nasty and bitter side of sibling rivalry is not inevitable. Many sibling conflicts are predictable and to a large extent preventable. Some, as we have seen, commonly occur around the time of the birth of a younger sibling and include an older child's reaction not just to the arrival of the new baby, but also to the attention the baby receives from family and friends and to his feelings when the mother is alone with the baby nursing. Other predictable sibling issues occur later on: conflicts over sharing toys, over a younger child's wish to be included in play when an older sibling has friends visiting. These too can often be prevented, and when they cannot be prevented, their impact can be greatly diminished.

Nursing and Jealousy

More and more mothers are choosing to nurse their babies, and for longer periods of time. Whatever the health benefits—and they appear to be substantial—this means that older children can easily feel left out during the times when their baby brother or sister is being nursed. This need not be, however. If your baby is not easily distracted while nursing, there is no reason why your two-, three-, or four-year-old cannot sit next to you while you nurse. Of course, some babies are more easily distractible, and some two-, three-, and four-year-olds find it difficult to sit quietly, so another strategy is required. One that has been helpful to many nursing mothers is the use of a *nursing box*. This is simply a box—often mothers and children decorate it with wrapping paper or markers and glitter to make it special—that contains small toys and snacks such as crayons and paper or pretzels and is taken out only when you need to have quiet moments with your new baby. Mothers who use this technique tell me that when they need to they will say to their older child, "Let's see what's in the nursing box today!" Your two-, three-, or four-year-old will feel special—after all, he has the nursing box toys to himself—and will be able to be in the room with you and the baby while playing quietly.

Expect Only the Kind of Sharing from Your Children that You Expect from Yourself

Whenever I am asked to speak about sibling relationship issues, whether it is to a group of parents or to a writer doing research for a magazine or newspaper article, there is one question I can predictably expect to hear: "What do you recommend parents do when their children do not want to share?" I often ask in response, "Why would we expect it to be natural for our children to behave so differently from us? Why would we expect them to share easily and graciously when we so rarely share ourselves?" We do not share our clothing, our automobiles, or our "toys," such as golf clubs, tennis rackets, or skis. We do not share our favorite coffee mugs with co-workers. We do not even readily let others write with our fountain pens. Why, then, should we expect our children to share their prized possessions? Of course, when posed this way, the question answers itself. The frequency with which the question comes shows how we can so easily project our own aspirations onto our children. None of us shared our toys the way our parents thought we should have. It will not help if we push our children into living out our fantasies of how this "should be." Unrealistic and unreachable expectations about sharing will disappoint and frustrate parents and children alike and lead to more, not less, sibling conflict.

What to Do about Sharing Conflicts

When two young children want the same toy—something that will inevitably happen despite your wishes—you can expect conflict, but it is not inevitable that the conflict will lead to screaming and yelling, to tears, or to physical fighting. There are some things that you can do to prevent the conflict from developing in that direction. The next time Lucretia and Natasha began to squabble over a doll, well before things got out of hand, Sally quickly reminded Natasha that the doll actually belonged to her sister. Because Sally realized that demanding that the true owner of the doll hand it over to her sister would be like asking an adult woman to hand over her baby to an admiring stranger, she felt comfortable being clear about this even in the face of Natasha's tears. Having seen what happened when she hoped they would resolve their differences themselves, she also was ready to intervene directly and forcefully. She knew that her two girls would not be able to work it out on their own.

After she stopped the squabble, Sally could have chosen to hand the doll to Lucretia, tell Natasha that the doll belonged to Lucretia, and be done with it. That would have at least temporarily ended the battle. But Sally wanted to do something that would have a longer-lasting impact. So she appealed to Lucretia's latent generosity: "Lucretia, this is your doll, and you don't have to share her if you don't want to, but your little sister is very sad right now. Can you think of something else you could let her hold for a few minutes?" Lucretia, like most young children, was really very sweet and generous when not panicked about being separated from her favorite toy. She immediately ran up to her bedroom and returned with a small teddy bear. Sally praised Lucretia effusively for her generosity: "That was very kind of you, Lucretia. Mommy really appreciates it!" You will find that this approach to resolving a conflict between two very young children will often succeed. When it does, you will have not only calmed down a near crisis, but given your child a chance to see how good it can feel to be helpful to a sibling, especially when parents take such note of it. Sometimes, however, the owner of the special toy balks at being asked to get another toy for her younger brother or sister. When this happens the simplest solution is for you to find something for your other child to play with.

Taking Turns

You should not demand that your children share their favorite and most special toys. But they can and should learn to take turns when playing a board game, sliding down a slide, swinging on a swing, or having the first bath. Because these situations are so different from sharing a toy, it helps to speak of them with your children as "taking turns" and not as "sharing."

Use Family Gifts to Teach Sharing

There is another way to teach the values of cooperation and sharing that you want your children to have, one that avoids the problems that occur when children are asked to share treasured possessions: Buy gifts that will be used by the whole family. Do not buy a train set, board game, or toboggan for one child, expecting that she will "naturally" play with it with brothers and sisters. If you really want your children to play with or use something together, buy it for everyone as a Christmas or Hanukkah gift, or just as a "family gift," telling them it is for everyone and keeping it that way.

If, however, you want to encourage generosity of spirit and action, you may do so by regarding sharing as an aspect of empathy and treating it as a special sign of caring, one that calls for special recognition: "I noticed how nicely you were sharing your toys with your brother. That was really great." Another useful strategy, one that recognizes the child's right to keep possessions to herself while offering some hope of averting a major battle, is to encourage the older child to share, not because "sharing" is somehow morally superior, but because it is a way to be helpful to Mom or Dad, a way that will be greatly appreciated. The regularly occurring scene involves two children under ten, one of whom may be seven or eight, the other anywhere between two and five. The younger child has grabbed the older child's puppet, bicycle, sweater, favorite animal toy, party favor, book, or crayon. The older is about to scream indignantly. What you can do is to approach your older child respectfully, not with authoritarian intent, but as one who wishes to offer guidance (influence is always more compelling than coercion).

"Naomi, do you have something else that you could let Matthew play with? Is there another toy that you could let Matthew hold for a minute? Matthew, look at this, Naomi will let you play with her other Beanie Baby when you give that one back to her. Matthew, that Beanie Baby belongs to your sister."

Be Authoritative, Not Authoritarian

Children who grow up in households that are either too lax or too punitive tend to have problems getting along with other children; this includes both siblings and nonsibling friends. Dr. Diane Baumrind, a developmental psychologist, conducted a series of important studies on the difference between permissive, authoritative, and authoritarian parenting styles. She found that young children respond best to very clear, specific, concrete instructions and that children who routinely receive instructions of this sort have better interpersonal relationships in all contexts. Children learn to follow instructions more quickly when parents are firm and when their instructions are unambiguous. "It's time for bed," "You must clean your plate if you want dessert," and "No more television tonight" are clear, specific, authoritative statements of the sort that young children understand best. They are reassured by knowing that guidelines and expectations are clear. Children whose parents are authoritative tend to have better self-esteem and better relationships with other children. They also are more self-confident and more assertive. These are all characteristics that tend to diminish intense sibling conflicts.

Statements such as "If you don't turn that television off right now, I'm going to destroy it!" "When I say jump, you ask, 'How high?!' " or "I'll show you who's the boss!" are authoritarian, not authoritative: they demand submission to greater force, not to greater wisdom. Children will yield, to be sure, but not without some later side effects. The most frequent such side effects are steep drops in self-confidence and assertiveness and a desire to be equally bossy with someone else, usually a younger brother or sister. Authoritative instructions make it easiest for children to learn what is expected of them: they are happier and better behaved when they know what they may do and what they are not permitted to do, what they must do and what they can choose to do or not. Rules such as "No between meal snacks" and "Once you are in bed you must stay in bed" are just a few examples of ways that parents can and should be the voice of authority: you are the ones who know what your children should do and when regular mealtimes should be.

Do Not Threaten: Take Action Instead

Andrea and Andrew's mother wonders why she has to scream at her children to get them to do what she asks: "They never listen until I scream at them and threaten; by that time we're all upset. How can I get them to do what I ask the first time?" This pattern is familiar to many parents. You ask your children to get ready for dinner. They continue to play, watch television, or ride their bicycles. You ask again, a bit louder this time: no response. You repeat the request, louder and with audible irritation in your voice; still no response. You shout, "If I have to say this one more time, you'll both go to bed right after dinner!" They finally respond.

Since this pattern is a cycle of sorts, all you need to do is interrupt it in one spot for the cycle to be reversed. Psychologist Dr. Gerald Patterson calls this pattern a *coercive family process*, and that is exactly what it is. Parents try (ineffectually) to get their children to follow an instruction, and children try (often with more effect) to avoid doing the same. The longer this goes on, the more established the pattern becomes: parents become convinced that the only way to get their children to respond is to scream and threaten; children learn that the only reliable signal that their parents are serious is when they scream and threaten. The standard threat "If you do that one more time . . ." is a good illustration of the problem, for the message it conveys is that the first time doesn't count.

The solution is simplicity itself: Follow through. If you ask your son to set the table and he does not, walk over to him, gently take him by the hand or arm, and lead him to the cupboard or counter where the dishes are; he will get the message much more clearly than with all the yelling in the world. And none of this needs to be unpleasant; all can be done gently and even with affection. You will find that you can communicate effectively with your children without yelling, and your children will learn to do as you ask the first time.

Conflicts over Friends

Another predictably difficult moment occurs when one of your children has a friend visiting and the other does not. Your younger child will predictably follow the older children around and want to play with them; your older child will predictably shout, "Mom! Alfie keeps bothering us!"

There are two approaches that may help. The first appeals to your older child's latent generosity and to her not-so-latent desire to please you. Before her friend comes over, take your child aside and remind her what a terrific big sister she is and how much you appreciate her kindness to her little brother. Tell her how much you will appreciate it if she includes little Alfie in her play with her friend. Believe it or not, this may actually work! If it does not, the strategy that is most likely to lead to success is to involve Alfie in a game or other activity, perhaps coloring or doing a craft project, with you or under your close supervision. Of course, this means that you will inevitably have to put on hold some things that are calling for your attention, but the fighting among the children will prevent you from doing them anyway. The choice is not between paying attention to Alfie or doing your other chore, but between paying attention to Alfie *before* a nasty eruption or after.

Know When to Intervene When Children Are Fighting

Another question I am frequently asked is, "Should I let my children work out their disputes on their own? When should I step in?" As with other similar questions, the answer to this one depends to a large extent on how old your children are. The advice to let them work it out on their own may be fine if your children are eleven or twelve or older, if they have good verbal skills, and if the dispute is purely verbal. Even under these circumstances, however, your guidance and assistance, if not your active participation, may be very helpful. By struggling through their issues basically on their own but with the benefit of your guidance, your older children may learn to negotiate and to compromise. These are important life skills. On the other hand, if your children are three, four, or five, they will benefit from your intervention for several reasons. First, you can help them learn the skills involved in negotiation and compromise. Second, and most important, you can keep them from hurting each other. Verbal arguments can quickly escalate into physical fights among young children: I believe it is a parent's responsibility to keep this from happening.

Temperamental Differences Are Important

Many of children's enduring ways of responding to events, people, and stresses are present during infancy and can be seen even in newborn babies (although newborn differences are often not stable). Pediatricians have known for many years that babies come into the world with their own ways of responding to it and to new experiences. In the mid-1950s Drs. Alexander Thomas, Stella Chess, and Herbert Birch began systematically to study and categorize these "temperamental differences." Their work has been continued by a number of developmental psychologists and developmental-behavioral pediatricians. Drs.

Thomas, Chess, and Birch described nine aspects of temperament: activity level, rhythmicity, distractibility, approach/withdrawal, adaptability, attention span and persistence, intensity of reaction, threshold of responsiveness, and quality of mood. After studying a large group of children for many years, Drs. Thomas and Chess wrote about a group of children they called "easy," who usually were in a good mood, whose bodily functions were regular, who reacted to most events with relatively low intensity, who adapted well to new situations, and who responded positively to the approach of a new person. They described another group of children with "difficult" temperaments who were in many ways opposites of the "easy" children. They were often in bad moods, had a hard time adapting to new situations, and often reacted to changes in intensity. They also identified a third group of children who were slow to warm up.

These *temperamental* differences continue to affect how children initially respond to new situations and new people as they develop, how physically active they are, how intensely they react to pleasant and unpleasant events, how sensitive they are to temperatures, textures, and tone of voice, and how readily they adapt to new situations. Very intense children often respond to change, disappointment, or frustration with intense emotional outbursts; they also respond with intensity to birthday parties, the first snowfall, and visits from grandparents. Some children are very active (this does not necessarily mean that they are hyperactive; see chapter 5); others have a naturally lower activity level. Some children greet strangers with enthusiasm, others with apprehension, and some with abject fear. Dr. Judith Dunn and her colleagues have specifically studied the ways that temperamental differences affect sibling relationships. They learned that easygoing and highly adaptable children adapted easily to the birth of a younger sibling; children with more challenging temperamental profiles tended to have more difficulty adjusting to their new little brother or sister. Each of these temperamental differences also has huge effects on how children continue to respond to their brothers and sisters. Easygoing children are easygoing about letting their younger siblings look at their picture books or hold their toys. Very sensitive and intense children react with great intensity to disagreements with their brothers and sisters.

Recognizing these temperamental differences can be extremely helpful to any parent who wonders, "Why are my children so different?" If one of your children cries and hides when a new baby-sitter comes for the first time and you know this ahead of time, you can arrange to have the baby-sitter arrive thirty minutes before you need to go out so that your child will have time to get used to the new sitter. If one of your children reacts intensely to any change from the familiar, you can help him become more adaptable by using a transitioning technique such as talking to him well in advance of any change in his routine and then reminding him ten minutes before the new event that it is coming. You may wish to use a countdown technique as well: "We're going to leave in nine minutes . . . eight minutes . . . one minute . . . ten seconds . . . nine, eight, seven, six, five, four, three, two, one!" If one of your children is very active and the other is less so, you can help them both find a happy medium in their play. Being aware of temperamental differences can help you tune in to each child as a unique individual. It can help you understand why the bedtime technique that worked so well with your older child is an abysmal failure with his younger sister, why one child shrieks in laughter when chased by a big brother while another cringes in fear. It can help you modify your approach in ways that fit each child, and it can help you guide your children as they develop, each one in a unique way.

Try This First When They're Doing It for Attention

Not long ago I visited a local family restaurant where I observed the following scene. A couple was sitting at the next table with their son, who appeared to be about four or five, and their daughter, who appeared to be about seven or eight. The children were playing in, under, and around the table. Then they began to chase each other around and to shout at each other with ever-escalating tones. They both climbed on a railing that separated two sections of the restaurant. The little girl then apparently had enough and sat down. Her brother could not calm down and began to push and pull on his sister's chair. Their father at first ignored this less than ideal behavior, then began to threaten his son with a series of probably unenforceable consequences.

Their mother, clearly distressed and embarrassed, said, "They're just doing it for attention." Of course she was right: they were doing it for attention, and they were getting it, too. How many times have you thought, "They're just doing it for attention"? If you are like most parents, the answer is "Many," and if you are like most parents, you have probably given them the attention they craved, because it seemed like the only option.

What other choice did the couple in the restaurant have? One thing they might have done was to notice and pay attention to good behavior, however small and however brief. They could have noticed that their little boy was occasionally actually sitting on his chair, and they could have given him attention for *that* instead: "Great job sitting, Harry! Look, honey, did you see how nicely Harry is sitting still waiting for his food?"

I am a great believer in trying the simple things first. One of the simplest things to try when a young child is teasing or chasing his brother or sister to get your attention is to give him the attention he wants so much, but to wait for a moment of good behavior and then give the attention for being good.

Here is a technique to use to prevent the next round of attention-seeking undesirable behavior. To give it a real try, you need to administer a full and strong dose of attention for being good. The standard I have adopted when counseling parents is to recommend that they find at least fifty things to acknowledge or praise each day for a week before deciding whether the technique is the right one for their child. Parents often ask what sorts of things they should be praising. The answer is anything and everything: putting on his shoes, clearing a plate from the table, looking up when you speak to him, putting on his mittens, drinking his milk, going to the bathroom, and any other activity that gives you an opportunity to catch him being good. The praise need not be verbal: a pat on the back or a ruffle of the hair is praise, too. Recognizing an activity also counts, especially for very young children: "You're painting with bright yellow now" or "You're really making that Lego building high!" Of course, this technique will not always work, but it works often enough, especially when the child is doing it for attention, that I recommend you give it a try.

Have Some Fun with Them!

Take time to enjoy your children. You will be happier, and if they are having fun, they'll be a lot more reluctant to risk giving up any of that fun because they behaved badly. This may strike many readers as terribly obvious, and I hope that it does. But I fear that we are all so caught up in the world of work—work at the office, working to be better parents—that we have forgotten that being parents is supposed to be *fun* at least some of the time.

If you put these suggestions into practice, you will be able to prevent some of the most common behavioral problems and sibling conflicts that occur in most, perhaps even all, families. If you prepare your older children for the arrival of a new sibling, keep your expectations for sharing realistic, adopt an authoritative parenting style, and be aware of temperamental differences in your children, you too will be able to prevent these common sources of sibling conflict from erupting.

Other sources of conflict are less predictable and thus less preventable. These are the conflicts that arise from and reflect the unique ways your children respond to situations, the unique ways you respond to your children, and the unique way *your* family works. These conflicts may not be predictable; they may not be preventable; but they can be diminished greatly even after they have begun by using some straightforward and practical techniques, techniques that you will read about in the rest of this book.

CHAPTER 2

Unfairness, Anger, and Sibling Rivalry

arriet and Dennis Stevenson were worried about the way ten-year-old David, their middle son, taunted and teased his little brother, four-year-old Jamie. In one day he teased Jamie about his Beanie Babies, shoved him off his chair, and put boiled peas in his milk during dinner just to make him cry. They knew that Jamie was not an angel but could see nothing he had done to deserve the merciless teasing and bullying that David rained on him. If this wasn't enough, David also avoided doing his homework in every way he could and complained that he hated going to school. Harriet recalled, "He just seemed so angry all the time. It started to get to us after a while. I started to get angry myself. No matter what we did he was never happy, and he was so difficult to be around."

Harriet and Dennis were doubly upset when David's second marking period report card concluded with this note: "David is a very bright boy, but he is not motivated to learn. He daydreams, fidgets, disrupts the class, and interferes with other children's learning." Harriet talked about this with Dr. Quince, David's pediatrician, when she took him for his regular checkup. Dr. Quince listened carefully, reassured Harriet that David was physically healthy, and suggested that Harriet and Dennis might want to consult a psychologist with expertise in helping parents whose children have behavior problems.

After an interview during which David said very little, the psychologist suggested some brief psychological testing. Dennis and Harriet agreed: "We worried that the doctor might tell us that there was something horrible going on, but we worried even more about not knowing." When they met with the psychologist after the evaluation, they were prepared to hear about problems, but they were not prepared for what they heard. Their son was dyslexic: he could not read. "All this time we were pushing and pushing him, and then we found out that he was really trying so hard and that he had dyslexia. We felt terrible."

Harriet and Dennis were educated people and thoughtful. They read everything they could find that might help them understand and resolve the conflict between David and his brother. The magazine articles and books they read told them that older children often feel that they are losing their parents' attention and love when a younger child is born, that parents must permit children to express feelings of jealousy, and that parents must learn to respond with compassion when an older child says he wishes his younger brother had not been born. They told David that it was okay to feel jealous and to be angry about having to share their attention. They talked with him about special activities they could do with him. One of the articles said that children may become so resentful of a younger brother or sister that they act out in school as well as at home.

Unfortunately, none of the books or magazine articles talked about the possibility that children who are having trouble in school may be so unhappy and so angry that they take it out on their siblings.

They talked with the psychologist about David's teasing of his little brother and the possibility that it might have something to do with his frustration and anger at not being able to read. Then they asked David: "When you pick on Jamie, is it because you are upset about something that happened in school?" They had to ask him several times, but David finally responded, "They make me feel dumb." Only then did they learn that David had been thinking of himself as "dumb" for many months, that he had assumed Dennis and Harriet were disappointed in him, and that this was the root of his anger, of his disruptiveness in school, and of his teasing of Jamie.

Like all parents who care about their children and who are trying to do the best for them, Dennis and Harriet felt guilty and sad when they learned that their little boy had been so unhappy for so long. They did not focus on these feelings for long, however, but took quick action. What Harriet and Dennis did shows how a few small changes in one aspect of a child's life can lead to big improvements in other areas, especially in his relationships with his siblings.

The first thing they did was to help David with his reading, the area of his greatest difficulty. They spent time after dinner reading with him and listening to him read, and they talked with him about his reading problem and his feelings about it. Dennis and Harriet told David how bad they felt that they had not realized how hard school was for him. They gave him credit for having tried so hard and told him that they now understood why he hated going to school and why he avoided doing his homework. They also told him that they felt bad that they had blamed him for being lazy when they should have been helping him instead.

Dennis had never talked about his own struggles in school out of embarrassment and from concern that this might send the wrong message to David about school and the value of learning, something he valued highly. When he learned of his son's struggles, however, Dennis decided that the time had come to speak up. He talked very directly about his experiences: "I had trouble learning to read, too. I remember that I thought I must be really dumb, but then I got some help. And I found out that smart people can have trouble reading, too. It turned out that I was one of those smart people. And it will be the same for you."

At first David pretended to be bored when his parents spoke with him. They sensed his caution and so stressed how serious they were, how truly bad they felt for misjudging him and especially for assuming that he was not making an effort in school when he actually was. At first David took advantage of the extra attention and sympathy to act out even more than before. His typical excuse was, "I can't help it. I have dyslexia." Dennis and Harriet made it clear that they were sympathetic and that they wanted to help him deal with his difficulty, but that they would not permit him to use it as an excuse for being disrespectful to them or to his teachers. Neither would they accept it as an excuse for being mean to his little brother. The combination of recognizing his difficulty, supporting him in his struggle to overcome it, and insisting on considerate behavior paid off. Over time David's self-image and mood improved considerably. Dennis and Harriet began to see real improvement in his relationship with Jamie. Before six months had passed, David stopped fighting about school or homework, and he was a much more pleasant son and brother. As a bonus, his reading skills improved considerably.

Much later Dennis said, "Looking back, I guess Dave's anger was a signal that something was wrong and that he needed help. I only wish we could have read the signal sooner. The problem was that we kept looking at the whole thing backward. All the books talked so much about jealousy being the cause of so many problems and how children who are jealous sometimes do badly in school that it never occurred to us that maybe the school problems came first. But now it makes sense that if he was having such a tough time in school, and especially if nobody noticed it or tried to help him—it makes sense that he would be angry."

When your child is nasty, negative, even outright hostile, toward a younger sibling, do not assume that it must necessarily be because he is jealous of the attention you pay to your younger or youngest child. It may be jealousy, but it may also reflect frustrations in other areas of your child's life, especially in school. Be especially alert to this if your child is also having academic difficulties. Ask him about it and be prepared to spend some time getting to the truth.

Why Do Children Talk about Fairness So Much?

Children talk about fairness all the time: in school, on the playground, in their neighborhoods, and at home. Their most troubling and intense complaints of unfairness always boil down to one of two strong feelings: "I'm doing too much and I'm not getting enough in return" or "Nobody realizes how hard things are for me compared to everybody else." When children are angry it is often because of feelings of unfairness. This does not mean that children are naturally selfish, but that they are very sensitive to imbalances in their lives and close relationships. We all want to be treated fairly at work and at home, by colleagues, supervisors, spouses, friends, and parents. Fairness concerns everybody, but we rarely stop to think about what we mean when we say something is not fair. In our most important relationships, as well as our work lives, we expect that there will be a balance over time between what we do for other people and how they respond to us. Although we do not talk about unfairness this way, what we usually mean is that something in our lives is out of balance.

One complication in thinking about children and fairness is that children often say, "It's not fair!" when what they really mean is, "I don't like this!" Preschool-age children complain that their bedtimes are too early, that they should be allowed to have dessert before eating dinner, and that their siblings got to sit next to Dad at dinner last time. School-age children may say that their friends all get to watch as much television as they want and are not expected to help with household chores. Teenagers complain that they are not allowed to stay out as late at night as their friends. These complaints often seem to reflect their disappointment that something has not gone their way, rather than what we adults would consider to be an unbiased judgment that a particular situation is unfair. At other times, children's complaints of unfairness and even their unexpressed feelings of unfairness are rooted in genuine imbalances in their lives, in their relationships with their brothers and sisters, teachers, and with parents as well. Telling the two kinds of situations apart is far from easy because a complaint that appears on the surface to be trivial or even concocted often disguises deeper concerns beneath the surface.

Eight-year-old Richard complained loudly, vehemently, and often that his ten-year-old brother, Paul, spent more time using the computer to play games than he did. This was no small matter to Richard; his complaints were rarely well reasoned or polite; his arguments were rarely voiced quietly; and his willingness to compromise was nonexistent. His parents were frustrated and angry about what seemed to them to be endless squabbling over a not very important matter. They had tried to resolve the problem. They made a point of involving both boys in decisions about the purchase of new computer games and made a sign-up sheet for them so that each would have equal access to the computer to play the games. Despite these efforts, Richard was unmollified and unmollifiable.

One day, his father in desperation sat Richard down and demanded an explanation, not unkindly, but very firmly, telling Richard that he knew something was bothering him and that he must talk about it. Richard fought this off at first, but when he realized that his father was going to wait as long as it took to get to the bottom of the problem, he broke down and in a flurry of upset, angry, and tearful words told his father, "Paul has lots of friends. He can go to their houses to play computer games. But I don't have any friends, so I should get to use the computer whenever I want to!" Richard's parents had not been aware of how different Richard was from his older brother and how he might need more help in socializing, how he, unlike Paul, let worry about what to say interfere with calling a schoolmate. They also realized that Richard was one of those children for whom making friends did not come naturally but required both effort and guidance. This realization took some time, since making friends seemed to be no more difficult for Paul than falling off a log. Once they realized that Richard needed help developing friendships just as other children needed help learning to read, they helped him in every way they could, by inviting other children over to play after school and on weekends, by reassuring Richard that other children did like him and that all he needed to do was approach them, and by giving him positive feedback about the nice way that he played with friends when they were over.

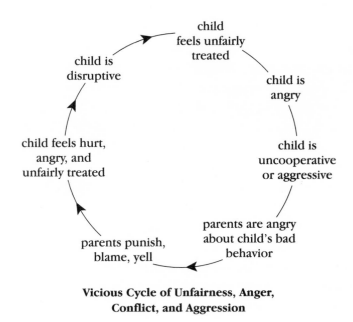

**Vicious Cycle of Unfairness, Anger,
Conflict, and Aggression**

Children's anger, whether expressed verbally or nonverbally, neither begins nor ends the family conflict that occurs when children experience unfairness. When children act badly, whether toward parents or toward siblings, we become frustrated, upset, perhaps embarrassed, and often angry ourselves. Parents often feel that the offending child should be disciplined, and parents are often right. But in the anger of the moment we do not always discipline calmly and with care. We are likely to raise our voices, to use sarcasm, to blame, to compare one child's evil deeds to another's heroic accomplishments or angelic devotion, or to be unfairly harsh and punitive.

All too often the result is a vicious cycle in which your child's experience of unfairness (perhaps the difficulty she has in school compared with the performance of her siblings), her anger about this unfairness, your anger, possibly your blaming or yelling, her hurt and anger at being blamed, and her increasingly disruptive behavior chase each other around in a circle with ever-increasing ferocity. Children become more and more angry and give their brothers and sisters, and parents as well, a great deal of flak.

Children Who Come into the World with an Unfair Burden

Children who have difficulties doing what other children can do easily, such as learning to read, making friends, or playing ball, rarely become philosophical about these difficulties. They get angry! They may look for someone to blame; the person they choose is often a younger brother or sister. Children who have these difficulties come into the world with an unfair burden: we should not be surprised if they feel that the world is unfair. Neither should we be surprised if they are angry. Yet, as David's parents learned, children respond to their parents' concern and efforts to improve their situation. The next story shows how children with other kinds of difficulties experience the same feelings.

Eight-year-old Michelle, the younger of Sandra and Tucker Stapleton's two children, was disabled. She wore braces on her legs, and walked only with difficulty. Her disability did not slow her down scholastically or socially: she was on the honor roll and had many friends. Her parents were perplexed and frustrated because she got so upset over what seemed like little things. Sandra said, "I'm not sure I can take this anymore. Two days ago she had an absolute fit. She couldn't have a friend come over after school because we had already planned to visit my sister. I tried to calm her down every way that I could. I told her, 'You can't change plans just like that without talking to people about it.' I tried not to yell, but it was very hard to keep my cool with her screaming and crying. She was totally out of control. She slammed the door when her brother was standing next to it. I was scared to death that his hand was in it. And we can't do anything about it. She takes it out on everybody, even her big brother, Gerry, and they're usually like that." Sandra held up two intertwined fingers. "When she finally calmed down—it was hours later—all she said was that the other kids wouldn't wait for her at recess and that she couldn't keep up with them."

We talked about the possibility that Michelle might have been angry about more than being left behind just that once, that she might be angry that she had to wear braces and use crutches while none of her schoolmates did, and that she might see that as unfair. When we asked her she said, "I am the angriest person in the world!" Sandra's eyes welled up when she heard this. She looked quietly at Michelle, unsure what to say. Finally Tucker said, "We're angry, too; we wish you didn't have to use braces. We wish you could run as fast as the other girls. It's okay for you to be angry." Afterward Tucker and Sandra said that they felt frustrated that they couldn't do anything to make life better for their daughter, that there was no cure for cerebral palsy. As we talked, however, they realized that they had done a great deal for her and that by talking with her openly about their feelings over her disability, they let her know that she did not have to keep her feelings to herself and that she did not have to handle them on her own.

After a while Michelle said something that totally surprised her parents: "I thought I wasn't supposed to talk about it. You always said I was just like everybody else. So I didn't say anything." Instead of saying anything, she kept her feelings to herself. Of course, Michelle could not keep her feelings to herself forever; she kept them bottled up as long as she could, and then she blew up, usually at home and often at her brother. When Michelle said this, her parents felt that they had made a terrible mistake by emphasizing her similarities to other children, by continuing to stress her strengths, and by telling her that she could do anything she set her mind to. They worried that they should have been acknowledging her limitations more.

But in fact they had not made a mistake. When she was a very young child Michelle had benefited a great deal from being told about her potential and being encouraged to do everything that other children were doing. Now, however, as an older child, her life and her feelings were different. The reality of her disability was more obvious to Michelle and to her friends than it had been when she was younger. It did stand in her way; it did make her different. So she had more need for acknowledgment of her disability. When Michelle started talking about her anger and her sense of unfairness, and especially when her parents talked about their feelings, too, it was as if some of the pressure had been released. She started getting along better with her brother; there were far fewer blowups.

Learn to Read Your Child's Emotional Signals

Children rarely get angry without reason. There are exceptions, of course, such as very young children who have temper tantrums or children who are developmentally delayed and unable to control their emotions as one would expect from children of their age. But most children have some reason for their anger. As parents we may not agree with their reasons, but we will always learn a great deal from paying attention to this anger and from trying to figure out what it can tell us about our children's lives and concerns. It is worth taking your children's anger seriously. Do not make the mistake of assuming that your angry child is "trying to get away with something," is "spoiled," or is "having another temper tantrum." These are, of course, all very real possibilities. Another equally real possibility is that your child is angry about something unfair in his life that you should know about and that you may very well be able to do something about if you know what it is.

What Every Parent Should Know about
How Children Develop

Children change so rapidly that even the most alert parent is sure to be left behind once in a while. This means that what worked last year, or even six months ago, will often not work today. One of the things that Michelle's parents and I talked about the most was how her emotional and interpersonal needs changed as she grew older. Some of the changes are obvious: children get bigger and stronger, they talk more and more clearly and use more "adult" language. Some changes, however, are hard to see. These are the inner changes: how children think about themselves, their feelings both about other people and about how other people respond to them.

You need not become an expert in child development, but it is important to bear in mind how rapidly your child's world is changing and to realize that some of these changes will inevitably arrive more quickly than you expect them to. All parents miss a beat on occasion and notice that their children have changed only after they find that the kind of reassurance, discipline, or explanation that was perfectly suited to a younger child no longer fits or works. When this happens to you, remember every child is unique and that it is impossible to anticipate every developmental change before it happens. The important thing is to be able to respond to the changes when you see them, as Michelle's parents did.

Why Children Act Up More at Home

"Joey's teachers say he's fine at school. Why does he behave so badly when he gets home? What are we doing wrong?" If this question occurs to you, ask yourself, "Is everything really fine at school?" Often everything is not at all fine at school; it only appears to be. Talk to teachers and others at school to find out what "fine" means. Does it mean "He's having some trouble with reading, but many other children are, too"? Does it mean "He's been teased a lot on the playground, but this sort of thing is beyond our control"? If it does, and it often does, Joey is not doing fine at all. Even if, as his teachers say, his behavior is not problematic at school, he may still be frustrated in some way that he does not express at school.

But the question still remains, "If he is unhappy at school, why does he act so badly at home?" Children always act out their frustrations and anger with people who they know will love them no matter what they do. No matter how caring and nurturing teachers are, children are well aware that there is a limit to what they will ultimately accept. Children also know that their parents, while they may become very angry and may punish them in some way, will continue to love them no matter how badly they act. Just as Joey brought his frustrations home from school each day, most children will relieve their frustrations not where they develop, but where it is safest to do so—at home. The converse, of course, is equally true. A child who is very unhappy at home but dares not express his unhappiness there may well carry it to school and demonstrate a remarkable repertoire of inappropriate behaviors.

What You Can Do to Address Fairness Issues

The way that Michelle's, Richard's, and David's parents handled these situations and helped their children provides guidance for all parents with a child who has angry outbursts, especially when they are aimed at an unwitting brother or sister. The first step is to recognize what your child's difficulty is, the aspect of her life that is unfair. Often you will be able to do this simply by listening carefully to what your child says. Sometimes, however, some input from a professional, such as the psychologist who evaluated David, can be very helpful.

The next step is to recognize that children need our help to cope with and overcome areas of life where they experience difficulties. Often parents believe that they are supporting their child's development and potential for independence when they downplay the impact of a difficulty, whether it is a marked developmental disability or a more subtle one such as a learning difficulty. It *is* extremely important to help children see themselves as capable, to emphasize their abilities, and to help them see that they can accomplish great things. But this does not mean parents should avoid facing the truth of their child's difficulties. Intense sibling conflict can be a red flag that your child is having a tough time in some area of his life. If you see this flag, gird yourself for the emotionally painful task of talking to him about it. You will almost certainly find what Michelle's, David's, and Richard's parents found, that your child has already thought about these things but has not wanted to say anything because of what he thought your response would be.

Take Your Child's Complaints Seriously

Ask yourself if your child's outbursts might be a way of showing you that something is unfair in her life. Even very young children are exquisitely sensitive to imbalance and unfairness, and surprisingly young children can tell you about it with some help. Remember that your child's aggression toward a brother or sister may reflect something about her life that not only seems, but actually is, unfair. David was angry that learning to read was so difficult for him and not for other children (or for his brother). Michelle was angry about the physical limitations she experienced as a result of having cerebral palsy. Richard was angry because his brother found it so much easier to make friends than he did.

When Relationships Go Out of Balance

Children can experience unfairness in life due to bad luck and other events that are no particular person's fault. They can also receive unfair treatment because of something another person has done to them or failed to do for them. The other person may be a teacher; it may be another child; it may be a brother or sister; it may be a parent. It is extremely important to try to sort out what is petulance, impatience, or limit testing and what is anger at unfair treatment.

The first thing that impressed me about twelve-year-old Jake Donnelly was how reserved he was. He entered the office tentatively, gently lowered his somewhat gangly five and a half feet onto my sofa, folded his hands in his lap, and waited. His sister, Emily, looked even younger than her seven and a half years. She was tiny in every respect, an impression that was heightened by her very fair complexion and pale yellow hair. The family was one of those unusual ones that fits the stereotype: Emily looked like her mother, Linda; Jake resembled his father, Fred. Linda and Fred, a minister and a pastoral counselor, raised their children to be kind to other people, especially to family members. They were distressed when the children's behavior was so far from what they had been taught. This is the way Linda expressed it: "They fight about what television station to watch as though it's the most important thing in the world. They fight about who gets the best seat in the family room when we watch a video together. It's crazy. On the way here they argued about who would get the front seat. I read a magazine article about sibling jealousy, but how could a twelve-year-old possibly be jealous of a seven-year-old?"

The answer emerged in a surprising way. After several meetings it turned out that Jake was having a tough time making up his mind about whether or not he dared to try out for his school's tennis team. The first thing he said was, "It's too much trouble." After a bit of prodding from his parents he admitted, "I'd kinda like to do it, I guess. I don't know." Finally he admitted that he was afraid that he might not make the cut, so he'd decided not to try. The other thing that emerged was that he felt that his sister, Emily, had a great deal in the family; she was so young that nobody expected her to do anything except "go to school, play with her friends, and be cute."

"Do you think that if you felt better about yourself, you might not be so eager to give your sister so much grief?" I asked.

"Maybe."

As I looked at Jake sitting there so composed and yet so tentative, it occurred to me that he might need a solid sign that his parents were on his side, that they were rooting for him. I said to Fred, "Maybe you could just go over and put your arm around Jake's shoulder, you know, to kind of say, 'We'll do this together, son.' " Jake's father's response was a soft-spoken and very simple, "I don't think I could do *that*; my family was never very big on that sort of thing."

And that, of course, was the problem: His family was not very big on demonstrating their concern or affection to anyone older than eight or nine, certainly not to a boy. Jake was angry not because Emily had no chores or homework, but because she was lucky to be considered young enough to be hugged once in a while. Emily was receiving lots of physical affection, while Fred was unable even to put his hand on his son's shoulder. So Jake was right: Emily did have a better deal in the family. She may not have been loved more or better, but she certainly was shown how much she was loved in a clearer way. Despite caring very deeply about his children, Fred was unable to see and respond to Jake's need for a clear show of support and encouragement, whether by a hug or in any other way.

Jake was hurt by a relationship imbalance: he was doing his best to achieve and to please his father, but his father was not doing an equal amount to build Jake up to withstand the possibility of failure or disappointment. Jake's situation was different from the others we have encountered in this chapter because its resolution required Fred to do more than identify Jake's problem and provide help for it. He had to change some things about himself. He had to look deeply at his own relationship with his son, at his assumptions about father-son relationships in general, and at his inability to be even a little bit demonstrative about his affection.

This work took some time and some effort, and it was not without discomfort on Fred's part. But when it was all over Fred said, "I always thought I was doing all I could for my children. Nothing in the world is more important to me than giving them each a good start, especially Jake. All I ever wanted was for him to have the self-confidence to try things, to believe in himself, but I never knew how to give him that extra support. If I'd known how much it meant to him, I would have been hugging him every day."

Of course, it was not just the hugs that made the difference in Jake, in his self-confidence, and in his relationship with his sister, all of which changed dramatically. It was Fred's attitude toward his son, his understanding of what was needed to really support his child's development; it was the whole and entire relationship between the two of them. When Fred changed the way he related to his son, Jake's way of relating to his sister changed, too. He no longer felt the need to comment viciously whenever she mispronounced a word. He no longer mocked her belief in the tooth fairy or made fun of her fondness for her favorite doll.

What can be learned from Jake's story? Perhaps the most important lesson is also the most difficult: sometimes when our children seem to be angry at their brothers and sisters, they are actually angry at us. Children's unhappiness at their relationship with a father or mother can show up in the ways they act toward a sibling. At its core Jake's anger reflected that he doubted himself and his ability to meet what he believed were his father's expectations. One of the most important things Jake said was that he would be nicer to his sister if he felt better about himself.

This story also highlights the importance of realizing that when children behave badly it often reflects an imbalance in our relationships with them. We are all aware of how important it is to us that our family lives be harmonious. It is just as important to our children. Children's relationships can either be balanced or imbalanced. When our children's efforts to earn good grades, to perform on the athletic field, to help out with younger brothers and sisters, and to make us proud of them receive our support, encouragement, and praise, our relationships are balanced. When our children's efforts receive our indifference or blame, our relationships with them quickly go out of balance.

When I first met them, Jake's relationship with his father was way out of balance. The emotional support Jake needed from his father was missing, and his behavior reflected this gap in his life. Later, after Jake's dad showed Jake how much he cared, after he worked to overcome his inherited prohibitions against hugging his son, the balance was restored.

Teach Your Children to Stand Up for Their Rights

Thirteen-year-old Amanda and her eleven-year-old sister, Linda, were very close when younger. Both wore their long blond hair braided into pigtails. They went for bike rides together. Sometimes they even wore identical clothes to school. They devoured the same dog magazines. They had begged and pleaded for a puppy for years; now that their family had moved to the suburbs they were finally able to have one.

They had promised to share equally in caring for the puppy as a condition of its purchase, but as time went on Amanda did much more feeding, watering, cleaning up accidents, and walking than she had expected—indeed, much more than was her fair share.

About six months after Clover became part of their family, Amanda started to become increasingly short-tempered with Linda: she snapped when Linda wanted to borrow a sweater or barrette; she glowered when Linda asked her to pass the salt. At first Amanda and Linda's parents had no idea what was happening; they only knew that the once friendly sisters had become enemies. Their mother put it this way: "It was as if someone turned a switch in the last six months. I used to be amazed by how well the two of them got along. You know, friends would complain about their children fighting, and we would just thank God that we didn't have that problem. Then boom, we did, and not just once in a while. It was all the time and every day, morning and afternoon, schooldays and weekends."

One evening Amanda's mother overheard an argument between the girls that helped her figure out both the problem and its solution. Amanda was yelling, "Linda! You never take Clover out after supper. You promised you would, but you never do!"

Linda yelled back, "I did it two extra days last week. You owe me!"

"I do not," said Amanda. "That was to make up for Sunday. You never keep your promises! I hate you!"

Linda whined, "Mom! Amanda's being mean to me! Make her stop." When things calmed down a bit, the girls' mother asked Amanda if she had become so nasty toward her sister because of the puppy walking. Amanda said, "I'm not being mean. Why are you blaming me, anyway?" After her mother convinced her that she wasn't blaming anybody, just trying to figure out what was wrong, Amanda said, "Linda promised to help with Clover, but she doesn't. She always has a million excuses. She has to do her homework. She can't find her gloves. Wouldn't you be mad?" After a long discussion with her mother, Amanda decided to confront Linda again about her responsibilities: "Linda, if you're not going to do your share of the work, then the puppy should be *my* puppy and sleep in my room every night." Hearing this, Linda decided that she would do more work, as she had promised. Amanda, feeling that fairness had been achieved, no longer attacked her sister as before: their previously friendly relationship was reestablished.

Much of what appears as jealousy, bitterness, and hostility between siblings—the worst of sibling rivalry—reflects what happens when a child's capacity to stand up for herself has been undermined, leading to feelings of unfairness and resentment. Babies and very young children are uninhibited in asking for, even demanding, what they need from others. Older children, however, become inhibited about making these direct requests. But this is not inevitable: parents can help their children learn to stand up for their rights, to voice their concerns, and to be assertive in the face of strong opposition. Younger children can learn that they need not give in just because a brother or sister is older. Older children can learn ways to resolve conflicts with younger siblings without resorting to bullying. Children who learn to be assertive in this way preserve their feelings of self-worth; they respect the rights of others in and out of the family; they do not need to find ways to "get even." The benefits of teaching children to stand up for their rights extend to relationships outside of the family. Once you have taught your children to stand up for themselves with their siblings, they will be more prepared to do so at school and in the neighborhood.

Parents sometimes worry that encouraging their children to stand up for themselves may lead to even more fighting. But there is a huge difference between healthy assertiveness and hostile aggression. Children who learn to be assertive have skills for resolving conflicts that make them less, not more, likely to be verbally or physically aggressive with either peers or siblings. Appropriate assertiveness reflects mutual respect and fosters dialogue. You can do a lot to help your children learn to stand up for their rights. Teach your children the difference between being considerate of other people and always doing what other people want them to, regardless of their own feelings and needs. Even children as young as six or seven can learn that just because a friend or sibling says, "You hurt my feelings!" does not mean they need to do what that friend wants. Help your children to state their wishes clearly and firmly. Your children will benefit from learning to be assertive in this way, and their relationships with siblings will improve just as Amanda and Linda's did.

The Cost of Giving Too Much

Twelve-year-old Molly was a sensitive youngster, one who was often mistaken for an older child, not because of size or physical maturity, but because of her extraordinary level of awareness of other people's feelings, especially those of adults.

Her parents' friends loved her, envied her parents, and regularly said so: "Molly is such a young lady; she's always polite and considerate; I wish our Vanessa were more like her." Her parents often told her how much they enjoyed her company and how impressed their friends were with her. This was a mixed blessing for Molly: she enjoyed it when her parents talked to her as to an adult; but she was so aware of their preferences, and so worried about their reactions, that she sometimes undermined herself. She did not talk about these worries but confided in her diary: "I'm not sure I always like it when EVERYBODY keeps telling me how grown-up I am. Maybe it would be easier to be like Adrianne and Ann Marie. Mom and Dad say how happy they are that I'm not moody or demanding, and I guess that's good, but I'm not sure."

Her father was teaching Molly to play chess. She was fascinated by the game and had been studying classic games and practicing against a computer program in her spare time. Her skills grew so rapidly that she could easily have won against her father much of the time if she really tried. But—and here was the problem—she did not try because she sensed that for her father this was a serious competition, one that he would be upset to lose. Another diary entry said, "I really like chess, but it scares me when Daddy gets so mad when we play. Last night he said, 'Look out! I'm going to wipe the board with you!' I just don't feel like playing anymore."

Molly's younger brother, Michael, had little of her sensitivity and none of her inhibitions. Despite having less skill, he managed to win one game in ten. Whatever their father's true feelings might have been, he praised Michael's skill and aggressive playing. This made Molly furious. She refused to play chess with Michael, refused to congratulate him on winning against their father, and actively looked for ways to make him feel miserable whenever she could. Their rivalry reached an all-time high. After a brief discussion with a family psychologist, Molly and Michael's father realized what he had been doing and became determined to change. He became very conscious of how she reacted to him.

He noticed that he did indeed become a bit downcast when she began to gain the edge. To his amazement, he also noticed how Molly's game regularly fell apart shortly after this occurred. He decided to talk with Molly directly: he admitted that he was very competitive and a poor loser, adding that he was very proud of her chess skills and that he bragged about her to his friends at work. He asked her to try hard to win and said that he would try to learn to be a more gracious loser. Finally, he said that he hoped she could learn to ignore his emotional reactions, that he wanted her to concentrate on the game, not on him. Of course, his request that she ignore his feelings was based on his knowing that she was so sensitive to begin with. This would not have been good advice for a child who was insensitive to other people's feelings, but it was great advice for Molly, as it is for any child who is too quick to feel responsible for other people's feelings. The result of this very serious and forthright talk was that Molly became a much more competitive chess player—her dad was now lucky to win a game—and a much more pleasant big sister.

Some children tend to give in too easily to their brothers and sisters—or, like Molly, to their parents. This is a tricky business because their giving in may at first appear to be generosity and to result from affection. And sometimes this is exactly what motivates the giving in. But when one child always gives in and another always gets what he wants, trouble is brewing on the horizon like a squall. This gets to the core of what it means for relationships to be out of balance. Balanced relationships are balanced because over time each person gets back a fair measure of what she has given. In parent-child relationships this may mean that we get to feel good as we watch our children mature into adults whose values we respect and whose accomplishments we admire. Among children in a family the balance is typically more concrete: "I let you watch your television show last time, now you should let me watch mine." The boy or girl who *always* gives in is not being generous or understanding, he or she is *overgiving*. Generosity is commendable and carries its own rewards, but overgiving leads to resentment, bitterness, anger, and inevitably to increased sibling conflicts.

Parents are often perplexed by a child who is sometimes so sweet and generous—who would do anything for a brother or sister, who is always the peacemaker, who always goes along to get along—but who sometimes suddenly turns irritable, or even vicious. The explanation may be that this child is not freely giving, but rather overgiving to his siblings.

Be willing to let your children win once in while, whether it is a chess or checkers game or an argument. Children who are afraid to win because their parents will be upset build up resentment that will be directed down the path of least resistance, usually at a younger sibling. The same is true of a verbal argument. When your child disagrees with you, as long it is done reasonably politely, do not insist that she look you in the eye so you can shout, "Who do you think you are?!" Rather, be proud that your child is learning to express her point of view, and say so.

Be Alert for Signs of Unfairness

The more tuned in you are to the balance of fairness in your children's lives, the more you can do to reduce anger and family conflict, and the more you can do to prevent its occurrence in the first place.

- When your children complain that something isn't fair, listen to their complaints seriously enough to find out if they have a legitimate gripe. This first sign of unfairness is the most obvious and the most often disregarded.

- Unprovoked aggression, especially if it occurs shortly after the end of the school day, often reflects frustration about what happened during the day. This is as true of preschoolers as it is of school-age children like David and Michelle.

- You should be concerned if your child avoids activities that involve competition or if she, like Molly, suddenly drops an activity in which she previously had a lot of interest.

- If your child has average or better intellectual ability but consistently does poorly in school, there are many possible explanations, such as a learning difference or difficulty or a problem paying attention. Another is that your child feels that his efforts are unappreciated or unacknowledged, that he is trying hard but no one cares or helps. Children who feel that the expectations placed on them are out of balance with their capacities to perform often refuse to work at all: the result is underachievement.

• If your child has very little energy, loses interest in doing things that she previously enjoyed, or is often tearful and sad, be sure to take these signs seriously. They often mean that your child is feeling that she cannot do anything that you value and appreciate. Unlike the child who becomes angry and blames you or a sibling, this child is blaming herself. You can help by identifying what she is doing or might do that both you and she can celebrate.

CHAPTER 3

Look for Each Child's Unique Abilities

Tim and Janice Appleton spent most of the little time they had together talking about what they could do to help their children (seventeen-year-old Andrea, fourteen-year-old Bill, eight-year-old Hannah, and five-year-old Mike) get along better. Andrea, Bill, Hannah, and Mike did not exactly fight. They never hurt each other physically: it was more constant cold war than physical battle. When Andrea won a leading role in a school play—she was infatuated with the theater and an aspiring actress—Bill could not resist the urge to say something sarcastic about how she probably got the role only because no one else was willing to be in such a "dumb play." When Bill, an enthusiastic but not especially gifted athlete, finally made the jayvee basketball team after trying for two years, Andrea got even by reminding him that the team was ranked last in the league and by asking, "Why is basketball such a big deal, anyway?"

The conflicts extended to the two younger children as well.

Bill and Andrea regularly teased Hannah about her clothes, her "babyish" interests, and her "dumb" friends. The teasing only escalated after Hannah brought home an A on a spelling quiz. Both Bill and Andrea had trouble with spelling and found it difficult not to feel jealous. Even Mike, the youngest child, was not spared. All three of his older siblings regularly complained about him to their parents: "Why doesn't he have to take out the trash or rake leaves? Why does he get to sleep in your bedroom when he's scared of a thunderstorm?"

Tim and Janice told me about a family dinner that characterized the conflict between the two older children. The arguing started as soon as Tim asked, "How was school today?"

Andrea, the first to respond, bubbled over with excitement: "Mrs. Dee put up the tryout results today. I got the lead!"

"That's great," Tim replied. "I remember how excited I was when I got my first big role. It was in *Arsenic and Old Lace*; I think I was in seventh grade."

Andrea stopped talking about her play and instead asked her father, "Who did you play? Did you have a lot of lines?"

She was immediately interrupted by her brother Bill. "Hey, Dad, guess what, I got a three-pointer today. The coach said I was doing great and if I keep it up, I might even be able to play varsity in two years."

Tim was about to ask his son to explain about three-pointers when Andrea chimed in, "We have this neat new makeup and you can put it on yourself. Mrs. Dee said that in the old days someone else had to put on your makeup because it was so sticky or something. Is that how it was when you were in school?"

"In junior high there was a makeup person, but when I got

to drama school we had courses in makeup and then we started doing our own."

Bill interrupted again. "Hey, Dad, this play stuff is boring. I wanted to tell you about the game."

Then Andrea jumped in: "Who cares about your stupid basketball, anyway?"

Not really knowing what to say, Tim took a shot in the dark. "Bill, look, your sister wants to talk about her part. Can't you just give her a minute before you complain that it's boring?"

But Bill couldn't wait. "But it is boring! Play this and play that, I'm sick of it! You never ask about my games. You hardly even go to the games anymore."

At this point Tim began to think, "What's going on here? Why can't they take turns? All I did was ask how school was. Maybe I should have stayed at work." He wondered why Bill and Andrea were always on each other like this. It seemed as if neither of them could resist the urge to say something critical or to put the other down. Tim and Janice were both terribly upset by all the fighting. They loved their children equally and tried to treat them equally. They wanted to know why Bill thought they were interested in his sister's theater activities but not in his athletics. And, they asked, if it was true that they had unknowingly favored Andrea, why did she continue to put her brother down at every opportunity?

The first thing we talked about was the possibility that Tim may have unintentionally detracted from Andrea's triumph by talking about his role in *Arsenic and Old Lace*. Tim said he had noticed that Andrea seemed to become more interested in his story than in telling him about her acting debut as soon as he mentioned his seventh-grade play. Instead of continuing to talk about how she won the big part, whom she was competing against, when rehearsals were going to start, and the thousand other details that he knew must have been on her mind, she had asked him about his role. Tim wished he had focused more on Andrea and her excitement instead of bringing up his experiences in school. He felt the same way about his comments about drama school and worried that they may have given Andrea the impression that he was trying to compete with her.

Tim also felt that he had missed an opportunity with Bill. He wished that he had responded when Bill complained that too much attention was paid to "plays" and not enough to his games. Tim knew he probably would not have gotten much of a response if he tried to talk to Bill about this at the dinner table, but he still felt it was a mistake not to have tried. What Tim really regretted, though, was having missed the opportunity to find out when Bill's next game was so that he could assure Bill he would be there.

Acknowledge Talents

The jealousy among the Appleton children shows how things can go wrong when children feel their parents are more aware of and impressed by their brothers' and sisters' accomplishments and abilities than their own. It also shows how even very well-meaning parents can easily contribute to this conflict without being aware that they are doing so. Tim's thoughts about his role in possibly contributing to Andrea's and Bill's jealousies highlight two points that will be helpful to all parents whose children seem to feel that a brother's or sister's special talents and special accomplishments matter more, count for more, and please their parents more than theirs.

First, do not leap from your child's excitement about something she has done to your reminiscences about your own achievements. Parents' comments about their own achievements, if habitual, can easily distort the nature of their relationship with their child into one characterized by competition rather than nurturance and support. When relationships between parents and children become competitive, the result is often that relationships between brothers and sisters become equally, often bitterly, competitive as well. Parents sometimes talk about their own accomplishments with the best possible intentions, in hopes that this will spur their children to greatness or because they think it shows their understanding of their child's experience. The problem is that talking about ourselves when our children are trying to tell us about *their* lives can easily make them feel that we're saying, "I don't want to know what's important to you. I want you to know what's important to me."

So when your children tell you about their accomplishments, take the time to share and enjoy their triumphs with them. Tell them how pleased you are about the achievement *and* how pleased you are that they wanted to tell you about it. Especially with older children and adolescents, it is important to recognize and acknowledge that sharing their accomplishment is a gift to you.

Second, action is far more effective in convincing children that their accomplishments are important to us than mere words can ever be. In their early teens, children begin to discount our praise: "You're just saying that because you're my mother." But they continue to pay a lot of attention to what we do. If you want to show your children that their sports activities matter, go to their games. If you want them to know that you are proud of their artistic accomplishments, go to their schools and look at the art exhibits.

Every child has a mix of abilities, talents, skills, and capabilities. Some accomplishments come naturally, some only with effort; others may be out of reach for some children even with very great effort. After all, only a very few children become Hollywood stars, chess masters, or concert violinists. But every child can do some things well: every child has unique abilities and strengths. The child who knows where her talents lie has a great advantage, one that will help her as a young child, as a teenager, and throughout adulthood. The girl or boy who knows where her or his talents lie is also much less likely to be upset, angry, or jealous about a brother's or sister's talents. This is especially true of children who not only know what their unique talents are, but who can see that their parents recognize, appreciate, and acknowledge these talents. Being able to do something that brings parents the glow of fulfillment and themselves the pride of accomplishment is essential to the development of children's self-esteem. It is also essential if children are to be able to celebrate their brothers' and sisters' accomplishments and good fortune. Children who know that they are recognized for their unique abilities are free to recognize their brothers' and sisters' abilities as well. Those who feel "I'm not good at anything" or "I'm not good at anything that Mom and Dad care about" will be more inclined to denigrate or undermine their siblings' good luck and happiness than to share in it.

Try Not to Be Defensive

Parents who have genuinely tried to avoid favoritism are always distressed when their children believe that they have favorites. When your children tell you that they know you prefer their brother or sister or that they doubt your love, your support, your recognition of their accomplishments, it is natural to respond by saying something like "How can you say that? You know that I'm very proud of you, that we love you all. You shouldn't feel that way." It *is* natural, but it hardly ever produces the hoped-for reassurance. Unless your child is merely trying to manipulate you (something that happens but is not as common as generally believed), he probably does feel that way. So instead of leaping to defend yourself against what may seem like an attack on your parental love, be curious. Try to find out what makes your child believe that you care more about his sister, would rather spend time with her, or appreciate her talents more. Children do not expect parents to be perfect and welcome the opportunity to enlighten us if they believe that we really want to know what they think and how they feel. This sort of discussion is never easy or completely painless, but the results make it worthwhile. If you can find out why your child thinks his sibling is the favorite, it will be much easier to know what to do to respond to his needs and to acknowledge his importance.

What Do Children Want?

Of all the many wants of childhood, none is more fundamental or profound than the desire to be able to give something of value to parents. Some of the seemingly cute things we have all seen infants and toddlers do are as important to their future development as learning to walk and talk. A twelve-month-old puts a Cheerios in his father's mouth; a sixteen-month-old tries to feed some of his egg to his mother; a two-year-old hands her blankie to her mother, who is in bed with the flu. These are the sorts of endearing things all parents have seen their children do, often thinking of them as examples of how cute and adorable very young children are when in good spirits.

Very young children *are* adorable much of the time, especially when they shower affection on you. But these cute behaviors show something much more important. They show that it is natural for children to want to be generous to their parents and to other people in their families. Examples abound in the daily life of families with young children. Four-year-old children regularly present their mothers and fathers with drawings, finger paintings, and other projects they have made at day care or nursery school. Older children continue to bring art projects home, adding spelling tests, book reports, essays, and report cards.

What do children want when they present you with these gifts? Most of all they want acknowledgment that they have done something that pleases you, something that makes you proud of them and of their uniqueness. If parents respond with appreciation to these generous efforts, children learn that they are valuable people who are able to contribute to their families and to others: they develop healthy self-esteem, and they learn to enjoy helping others. One of the easiest and most powerful things you can do to foster the growth of self-esteem and generosity is to recognize and acknowledge these contributions clearly and sincerely, not just the athletic and academic achievements of teenagers, but also the gifts of the very young. Thank your toddler for sharing his cookie. Thank your preschooler for putting her favorite stuffed animal on your bed to keep you company when you have the flu. And be sure to express your appreciation as seriously as they expressed their concern and generosity. Remember that very young children do not think of themselves as cute when they give us these gifts any more than we think of ourselves as cute when we give a close friend a wedding gift.

Celebrate Differences

Children live in a very competitive world. Much of the typical school day emphasizes competition, and children soon become aware of this whether or not their parents explicitly push them to the heights of achievement. It is very easy for well-meaning parents to communicate great expectations without meaning to do so. Children are typically very sensitive to every nuance of what their parents say. The next time you are tempted to talk about your amazement at the wondrous and well-publicized achievements of twelve-year-old pilots, fourteen-year-old college students, and sixteen-year-old circumnavigators, look carefully at your children and ask yourself if it is just possible that they might think you expect these kinds of accomplishments from them, too. Be sure to let them know that you know the difference between the entertainment value of activities that make it into *People* and the things that really matter to you.

Parents can also communicate disappointment as much by what they do not say as by what they do say. Some time ago I worked with Judith and Charles Johnson and their two sons, seventeen-year-old Chuck and eleven-year-old Dave. Charles often bragged to his friends at work about his sons' achievements, but he never repeated this praise at home, where they could hear it. Instead he regaled his family with stories that his co-workers had told him about their children's accomplishments. One evening, for example, he talked about his friend's son who had won a scholarship to Harvard. Dave was a bit young for this to have much meaning, but for Chuck the message seemed clear: his father wished that Chuck could be more like that Harvard-bound boy. Chuck took it to heart, felt both sad that he had not met his father's expectations and angry that he could not be acknowledged for his own accomplishments. Neither Charles nor Judith imagined that Chuck took every remark so seriously; neither noticed his mood change; neither asked him what he was thinking or feeling. When Charles became aware of the effect that his stories were having on his son, he not only stopped telling them, but began to tell Chuck how proud he was of him and how he had bragged about him to his friends. Chuck's self-esteem began a gradual climb back to a healthy level, and his mood and attitude improved as well.

Be Enthusiastic

A parent's enthusiasm for one child's chosen activities can stand in marked contrast with his polite interest in another child's activities, leading to hurt feelings and considerable conflict. Many years ago I was consulted by Alexander and Elizabeth Pearson, who were concerned about the conflict between their two youngest children, fifteen-year-old Lew and thirteen-year-old Lavinia. Lavinia's life centered around sports, especially soccer. Lew was passionate about art and hoped to study painting at Pratt Institute after graduating from high school. Alexander Pearson was a sports fan of the first order; he enthusiastically attended all of Lavinia's games, drove her to soccer clinics, and talked with her about possibly gaining an athletic scholarship to a prestigious college. He thought that he was being supportive of Lew. He told Lew that he should pursue his own interests and that he should not feel any pressure to play sports if he did not want to. He did not, however, take Lew to New York to visit museums, as Lew had frequently requested; neither did he read the art books that Lew gave him. When Lew talked about a painting he was working on or about a technique he was trying to master, Alexander's response was one of polite boredom.

Alexander said that art museums were all very well for those who enjoyed them, but that he was not one of those who did. Although Elizabeth encouraged Lew's artistic endeavors and was happy to accompany him to museums, Lew still longed for more support from his father. As we discussed this issue, Alexander had a change of heart. He realized that going to a museum with his son did not require that he be especially interested in art, only that he be especially interested in his son. Since he was truly interested in Lew and in Lew's education and future happiness, shared museum trips as well as discussions about art became enjoyable for both father and son. Lew's relationship with his father improved dramatically, as did his relationship with his sister.

Identify Strengths

Scholastic achievements are easy to talk about; they are concrete; they are familiar; they are undeniably important. But parents who want to acknowledge each child's importance as a unique human being will look for strengths and talents in all areas of life. The first step to helping children recognize and appreciate their own uniqueness, including their unique abilities, is to observe them in as many situations as possible. Of course, all parents watch their children; and all parents listen to their children. This is watching and listening with a special purpose, to find out what really excites them, what stimulates their creativity, what stimulates their sense of self-worth, and what kind of giving to their parents comes to them spontaneously. The more you can learn about your children and the earlier you can start to do so, the more you can help them identify those interests and abilities that will give them the self-confidence that does so much to foster cooperation in the family.

When Anna was just three years old she saw a television spot for an upcoming performance of the *Nutcracker*. Entranced, she asked her father, "What's that?"

"It's ballet," he responded. "Would you like to try it someday?" When Anna said that she would, her parents took her to a local dance studio to watch a children's ballet class. Anna was so fascinated and so eager to dance herself that they enrolled her in a dance class for three- and four-year-old children. It would have been easy to dismiss a very little girl's interest as unimportant, but by taking her interest seriously, Anna's parents helped her discover a love of dancing that remains a very important part of nine-year-old Anna's life today.

Acknowledge Your Children's Accomplishments without Comparing Them

In looking for and acknowledging each of your children's strengths, avoid the temptation to compare them. From the moment of Aaron's birth his parents compared him with his older brother. Jason had been extremely active at birth; Aaron was placid. Jason was difficult to soothe; Aaron was easily calmed. Their parents meant no harm; it seemed natural to compare two boys who were only eighteen months apart. It probably would not have done any harm if the comparisons had been limited to infancy, but the pattern proved difficult to break. By the time I met Aaron and Jason they were eight and ten, had been compared all their lives, and had been fighting for nearly all of their eight years together. Their parents were committed to doing everything possible to reverse this situation and, after many months of very hard work, were able to do so. They made a point of acknowledging Jason's energy and enthusiasm for every activity in which he was involved. They strongly acknowledged Aaron's quiet persistence and composure when faced with difficult challenges. They rigorously avoided any comparisons. When things were finally better they both said that they wished they had known to avoid comparisons when the boys were babies, that it would have spared them all a lot of pain.

. . .

Shirley Jansen felt that she was acknowledging her children's unique personalities when she told her daughter Rachel, "You have always been the creative one; Ruth is more the people person." Unfortunately Shirley was actually introducing comparison, and thus competition, into the relationship between the two sisters. Neither Rachel nor Ruth was pleased by being characterized this way: each thought that the characteristic attributed to the other was more desirable; each felt that her mother favored the other sister. All Shirley needed to do to markedly decrease the competition was drop the comparisons. She continued to praise Rachel's creativity; she continued to recognize Ruth's interpersonal sensitivity, but she stopped comparing them. Free of the burden of being compared, Rachel and Ruth were able to enjoy their mother's recognition of their unique strengths without feeling they had to compete.

The mother who told her son, "Not everybody can be a great student like your brother; you have your music, and that's fine," intended this to be reassuring. It was not. The comment about music came off as a weak and backhanded compliment; the remark about not being a great student hurt terribly; the comparison fueled the already raging fires of competition between the brothers. What this mother should have said, and what she did say later, was, "I love listening to you practice your cello; it makes me feel good that you get so much pleasure from it." This second statement did what the first could not; it recognized her son's musical abilities and interest without comparing him with his brother in any way. All comparisons, even positive ones, have two problems: they pigeonhole children, limiting their freedom to discover for themselves who they are, what attracts their interest, and in what areas they have the potential to excel. They feed competition among siblings. We can recognize our children's unique capacities if we acknowledge who they are and what they can do without any sort of comparison.

Try Out Your Child's Point of View

Let's consider some other examples of parents' attempts to be positive and how using just a few different words can make a big difference to a child. The key is to make your recognition and praise honest and realistic. Overblown praise can cause your child to doubt your sincerity and thus be worse than no praise at all. Joseph Beels was very proud of his eight-year-old son Joey's intellectual accomplishments and was fond of saying things like "You're much smarter than I am," thinking that this was the highest form of recognition. Little Joey was proud of his ability to read and pick up new ideas quickly, but he certainly did not think he knew as much as his dad. He was uncomfortable when his dad said these things, even to the point of worrying that his dad might feel bad about having a son who was smarter than he. Joseph was puzzled that his son did not seem pleased when he received this sort of praise. A very small adjustment solved the problem. In the place of his previously grand statements, Joseph told his son, "I'm really proud of the way you read so well," and, "It's great to watch you catch on to things so quickly." This acknowledgment fit with Joey's experience and with his view of himself; he understood it and was very pleased by it.

. . .

If we say to an eight-year-old, "What a terrific artist you are. I bet you could win a competition, and wouldn't that be great!" we are unintentionally implying that the only reason to do art is to win a competition. This is fine if the child does indeed win not only that competition, but lots of others, too. On the other hand, if we say, "Your drawings are terrific; it makes me so proud that you are creative in this way," we have preserved the positive part of the message and edited out the negative, the part that might undermine the positive, supportive, and acknowledging aspect of what we wish to say.

Each of us has a unique way of looking at things, and our children are no different. This is especially true of children's activities. A two-year-old is pleased by the process of scribbling with a crayon, the way it feels in her hand, the patterns of the colors on the paper. A five-year-old gains pleasure from drawing a picture of something she especially likes: perhaps herself, perhaps her dog or kitten, perhaps her family. At eight or nine, many children begin to focus on improving their skills. "Is this drawing of the puppy more realistic than the one I did last week?" they wonder. At each age the child enjoys her drawings, yet she will respond most positively to varying acknowledgments. The kind of acknowledgment that will have the most meaning, that will help the child grow the most in self-esteem and self-worth, and that will help the child feel important enough to be able to reach out to a brother or sister will be the acknowledgment that fits best with how she sees herself.

Learning to adopt your child's point of view will give you a wonderful tool, one that will help you add to your child's emerging sense of self and sense of self-worth in many ways and at many times. Fortunately it is not that difficult to adopt a child's point of view. We need only follow our children's leads, or at least be certain that we do not get too far out in front of them. Talking about applying to Ballet Russe with a five-year-old who loves her ballet class and comes home twirling and chatting happily about third position is an example of getting too far out in front. Watching while she demonstrates third position and listening carefully as she describes what she did in ballet class, on the other hand, is an example of carefully following her lead. Telling an eight-year-old aspiring Little League pitcher that with hard work he may be able to win an athletic scholarship is another. If that same eight-year-old asks, "Did you see my last pitch? Wasn't it great! Do you think I could play with the Yankees someday?" you will want to respond differently.

Your Dreams May Not Be Their Dreams

All parents have hopes and dreams for their children. Some of these hopes carry with them the wish that our children will be like us, perhaps that they will follow our paths in business, a profession, or another career. Or we may hope that our children will accomplish what we have not been able to. The desire that our children will in some way enjoy achievements, comforts, accomplishments, or accolades denied to us is an undeniable aspect of being a parent. Yet these wishes are not without risks: we may unknowingly impose our feelings, our hopes, our wishes, onto our children. Perhaps their personal aspirations will mesh with ours, and the result will be mutual gratification. But what if our son or daughter is inclined in a very different direction from the one we would choose?

. . .

Ian and Jackie McDougal had two daughters, twelve-year-old Shelly and fourteen-year-old Nadine. Ian was a painter; Jackie was a surgeon. Whenever Shelly or Nadine wanted to talk about their futures, where they might like to go to college, what they might like to major in, or possible career paths, Ian and Jackie would say, almost in unison, "Don't worry about those decisions now; there are lots of interesting medical specialities to choose from." Jackie's reason was perhaps evident; she enjoyed her career and had been very successful in it. Ian's reason for making this statement was a bit more complex; he had never wanted to be anything but a painter. His work was well respected, but he had made very little money from it. He saw medicine as a not very exciting but very secure way to ensure a good income.

But neither Nadine nor Shelly was especially interested in the idea of a medical career. Nadine wanted to be a painter like her father; Shelly loved to cook and hoped to have her own restaurant someday. Ian wanted to be supportive of Nadine, but thinking of his daughter trying to make her way in the very competitive art world made him anxious. Despite earning excellent grades and being active in church and community activities, both girls felt there was nothing they could do to earn their mother's respect and admiration unless they gave up their dreams and studied medicine. As they progressed further into adolescence, they grew more and more unhappy and more and more unpleasant to be around. After much soul-searching and family discussion, Ian and Jackie realized that they had been pushing their children to follow Jackie's professional path without being sensitive to what Shelly and Nadine wanted. As Jackie and Ian were more and more able to listen to their daughters' hopes and aspirations, and even to their anger at being pushed in the one direction, Shelly and Nadine seemed gradually to change. They more often talked spontaneously to their parents about their interests; they squabbled less often with them and with each other.

When parents impose their dreams on sons and daughters, the children can easily feel like failures despite their actual successes, and feeling like a failure is the surest route to looking for the first opportunity to make a brother or sister feel like a failure, too. If parents naturally have these dreams and ambitions, can we simply jettison them with no more thought than if they were so many empty barrels? I do not think so. But we can try as hard as possible to make our highest priority the recognition of each child's unique interests and abilities, relegating our personal ambitions to a distant second place. We may even find that we can fulfill some of our long cherished ambitions ourselves. If you have always wished that you knew how to play the piano, and your daughter has neither musical talent nor interest, don't force her to practice; take piano lessons yourself. If you have regrets that you did not expect enough of yourself in the past, start to set your sights higher instead of compensating by raising the high-jump bar for your son.

Children of all ages need to see that you appreciate their efforts, even if these efforts do not always meet with success. Knowing what to say and how to say it is a tricky business at best: it is important to remember that you will not get it right every time. Parents need to acknowledge their own efforts, too. Here are some general rules that may be helpful. Each of them has two purposes: to increase your children's self-confidence and self-esteem and to sharply decrease the nasty side of sibling rivalry.

• *Do not confuse criticism with encouragement.* If you are teaching your seven-year-old to row and she dips the oars too far in the water—"catching a crab," as the old salts say—do not bark out, "You're catching a crab!" unless you aspire to be the next Captain Bligh. Try this instead: "You're getting the idea; you're holding the oars just right; you're keeping them in the oarlocks, too. Maybe next time we could work on twisting the blades so they enter the water smoothly—that way you can go a little faster."

• *Remember that sarcasm is not a form of humor.* It is a form of insult, and no one is more aware of this than a child. When your son or daughter drops the ball, do not say, "Great hands." You will wait an eternity for the laughs. If the laughs come at all, you can be sure they will be from a sibling, happy to see someone else on the receiving end of this sort of barb.

• *Never compare your children to each other, to your neighbors' children, to your nieces and nephews, or to yourself as a child.* Children are compared so much in school and among their peers that any hint of comparison from parents, even if well intentioned like Tim Appleton's comments about his acting or habitual like Charles Johnson's stories of his co-workers' children, will inflame an already tender spot on any child's self-esteem.

• *See your children for who they are.* Help them to find their unique interests and abilities, whether or not they overlap with yours. Don't insist that your daughter play the cello because you love Yo-Yo Ma or because you wish that you could have taken cello lessons as a child. On the other hand, if your daughter falls in love with the cello the first time she sees Yo-Yo Ma on television, remember how the parents of the little ballerina responded to her fascination with the *Nutcracker*: nurture her interest and help her find out if it is one she wants to pursue.

• *Try not to be defensive.* If your child says that he feels you are disappointed in him, try to find out why he feels this way before telling him that he shouldn't. You may learn something valuable, and he will know that you take his concerns seriously.

• *Avoid put-downs.* What parent knowingly puts his or her children down? But parents who were put down a great deal themselves may use put-downs so much that doing so has become habitual. Don't tell your child, "You're so clumsy," "You run like a turkey," "You're a terrible swimmer," or "What an awful French accent." Whatever a parent may intend by such comments, the effect is that of undeserved punishment, and one thing we can be certain of is that punishment of this sort will make your children feel bad about themselves, angry at the world and at their brothers and sisters: it may quite probably lead to more intense, nasty, and protracted sibling rivalry.

• *Listen to your children.* This is one thing that you can do for your children that costs no money, that produces immediate and long-lasting results, and that very few people can do for them as you can.

CHAPTER 4

Give Credit Where Credit Is Due

Eleven-year-old Tommy Richardson and his fifteen-year-old sister, Allison, lived in a small town about twenty miles from the state capital. Tommy and Allison's older sister, Janice, was majoring in sociology at the state university on a full academic scholarship. Their mother was a nurse. Their father owned the local hardware store. Tommy loved sports and had lots of friends, but he hated school. Like Janice, Allison earned top grades in school. Tommy's parents saw no reason why he shouldn't do the same. They tried to help by meeting with his teachers and monitoring his homework, but they did not soften their expectations that he earn the same grades as his sister. Tommy complained that the work was just too hard, but his parents could not accept the idea that he might not have the same abilities as his sister. Instead of praising him for trying, they blamed him for not doing better.

Tommy was terribly hurt by this criticism. He did not say anything about it to his parents, instead taking his anger out on his sister. This was all the more striking because the two children had been so close when they were younger. Allison had doted on her baby brother, and he in turn had adored her, not just when he was an infant and toddler, but right through second grade. Now, however, he got on her nerves in ways that only a younger brother can, by listening in on her telephone calls, by enthusiastically telling her boyfriend about the pimples on her chin, and by "accidentally" splashing ketchup on her blouse.

Tommy's parents tried everything they could think of to resolve this situation and asked advice from every family member who might be able to help. Uncle Hank thought that Tommy might be going through puberty early and that his behavior toward his sister was preteen moodiness. He advised Tommy's parents to wait for him to "grow out of it." They were initially reassured by this but quickly decided that it would not be fair to Tommy or themselves to just wait it out. Besides, they wondered, "What if he doesn't grow out of it? What if it gets worse?"

Then Tommy's mother talked to her sister, a teacher in a Chicago suburb. Of all the people they had talked to about Tommy, his aunt Sally was the first to ask about Tommy's school life. His father said, "We never even thought about the possibility that Tommy might be having trouble with schoolwork. His teachers always said he was very bright, just not well focused. We thought they were trying to find a nice way to say that he's lazy." Sally saw it differently, told them about the many times she had seen teachers blame a child for being unmotivated when he was actually struggling to keep up, and suggested they find an expert outside the school to help them find out if Tommy was really lazy or not. Tommy's parents followed

Sally's advice and consulted a child psychologist, who evaluated Tommy and explained that his abilities were solidly average and that he had actually been working very hard to earn C's in his academically challenging school.

At first Tommy's father was angry. "There's no way that any son of mine is average!" Later, after digesting the new information, he said, "We'll just have to adjust what we expect of him." Tommy's mother added, "We were upset at first, but then I said, 'Look, at least now we know he's trying; that's the most important thing.' " Tommy's parents made real efforts to compensate for their previous unfair criticism of their son. They told him how bad they felt that they had not given him credit for his hard work. They immediately talked with his teachers, emphasizing that he had been working very hard all the time and should not be criticized for being lazy or slacking off. More important, they did all they could to show him that they appreciated his efforts now that they were aware of them. They frequently told him how pleased and proud they were that he was trying so hard and made sure to praise him for his excellent spelling. When he had a big project his father sat at the table doing paperwork while Tommy worked on his project.

Since Tommy had been unhappy in school for so long, his parents were not surprised that it took some time for him to turn around. But turn around he did, both in his attitude about school and in his relationship with Allison. She was suspicious at first, "He's only stopped being a pest because he wants something from me." After two months, when the "new Tommy"— actually a rebirth of the "old Tommy" with whom she had been so close for so many years—was still there, she began to soften. When Tommy took a chance and asked her to help him with his math homework, Allison was cautious, afraid a battle would erupt. But when her mother encouraged her to try it out, Allison did so in a way that was more helpful and nurturing than anyone would have expected. She asked Tommy what he wanted to work on, reassured him that she too had things that were very hard for her in school, and made sure that they ended their study time with a success.

Tommy's parents blamed themselves for not being able to see Tommy's intellectual abilities accurately and for assuming that he was gifted when he was not. They should not have been so hard on themselves. It is extremely difficult to estimate a child's intellectual abilities just by observing him. Even highly experienced child psychologists are sometimes wrong in their first guesses about a child's abilities: that is why they use standardized tests. It is even more difficult for parents to accurately estimate their children's abilities under the pressure of receiving poor report cards or complaints from teachers. No parent should expect to tell with any degree of accuracy whether their child is "really trying hard" in school.

Allison was an unusually caring and sensitive sister, and the bond between her and Tommy prior to the school difficulties that began in third grade was unusually strong. It would not be fair to suggest that parents should be able to turn around every instance of conflict between an older sister and a younger brother in such a dramatic way. We can, however, learn a great deal from the process that Tommy and Allison's parents went through in resolving the conflict between their children, just as we can from their reflections on their mistakes. Tommy's mother said, in musing on her experience, "I wish somebody had helped me see that other things can be just as important as grades. But that was always the big thing when I was a kid. Neither of my parents finished high school, and they always pushed us to spend more time on our studies. They always emphasized that education is the best way to get ahead. And I guess it worked, since my sister and I both graduated from college. One of the things I've now learned from her is that some very bright and hardworking kids have a lot of problems later on because they don't know how to get along with people, but Tommy is great at that. I just read some studies that said that emotional intelligence is more important in success than what grades you get in school. I am just glad that we saw the light before it was too late. Tommy is so much happier now. And the great thing is that his grades have actually gone up a bit."

Recognize Efforts to Achieve in School

All children feel hurt and angry when they try hard to accomplish something that is difficult for them but receive no recognition for their efforts. The anger is often directed at their brothers and sisters. The approach taken by Tommy's parents can be applied by any parent. They made two basic mistakes, caught them, and took action. Their first mistake was one made by many parents: they forgot how important school is to children and how pervasive is its impact on all aspects of a child's life, including his sense of self-worth, moods, and relationships with parents and siblings.

School occupies the same role for children Tommy's age that work does for adults, and a bad experience at school can truly be devastating. Imagine going to work every day filled with dread that you will be criticized for doing a poor job. Imagine going to work every day worried that you may be fired. Imagine going to work every day feeling that you failed the day before and worrying that you will fail the next day as well. This is what life feels like for children who have difficulties in school. It is what life feels like for children whose teachers are overly critical and lacking in patience—it is just the same as having a bad boss. So when you see a change in your child's mood, her way of responding to other family members, or her behavior, the first two things you should think about are "What has been happening in school?" and "How is my child feeling about herself during the school day?"

The Risk of Assigning Motives

The second mistake Tommy's parents made was in believing they knew *why* he acted as he did without asking him. We all do it. We think we know why someone else has done something we dislike. We do not bother to ask the person why *they* think they did what they did, or we ask but do not believe the answer. Often our beliefs, like those of Tommy's parents, echo those of our children's teachers. Sometimes we form our beliefs based on our experiences with our other children, as Tommy's parents did. Be very careful before assigning motives to your children that you would not want assigned to yourself, especially if you truly do not believe they would fit you. If you know you are motivated and hardworking, it is unlikely your children will be lazy, since they have had the value of work modeled for them all their lives. Rather, it is more likely that something else is going on that makes it look as though they are lazy.

Teachers, unfortunately, cannot produce an X ray of a child's mind any more than parents can: all they can do is share their observations. So if your child's teacher tells you, as did Tommy's teacher, that he appears distracted, restless, and not focused on his work, consider *all* the possibilities. One possibility is laziness. An often overlooked but very frequent cause is a previously undetected learning difficulty. Tommy's parents realized that this was a possibility and took action by arranging for an evaluation of his intellectual and academic strengths and weaknesses. Another, invoked all too often but still worth considering, is a neurologically based problem with attention and concentration. Another, especially among very bright children, is boredom. An eleven-year-old girl once told me that she could not understand why the teacher talked so much in math class when they were doing basic algebra: "The answers sort of leap off the page at me. I only listen to the teacher when she says something that isn't in the book."

Understand Your Child's Scholastic Strengths and Weaknesses

Marty Evans was ten years old and totally miserable in school and at home when I first met him. He fought not only with his older brother and younger sister, but with his parents as well. In fact, Marty would pick a verbal fight with anyone at any time. Marty's parents were well aware that his understanding of spoken language and his ability to use spoken language was more typical of a bright college student than of the ten-year-olds in his fifth-grade class. Not only were they aware of this, but they praised him for it at every opportunity. But Marty was one of the relatively small number of children who are terribly bright and yet struggle to learn in school because of the way they learn. Sometimes a child's natural approach to learning is so different from that of the typical child that classroom teachers are not equipped to teach that child effectively. In these instances a learning difference becomes a learning difficulty.

Marty's particular learning problem was that he had a very difficult time with reading. Since reading is such an important part of a school curriculum, he felt like a big failure most of the time. When he and I talked about this he said, "I know you think I'm smart, I know my mom and dad think I'm smart, but I don't *feel* smart." Marty's parents and I worked hard together to find some ways that Marty could shine at school so that he could come home feeling like a winner instead of a loser. When Marty started listening to college-level books on tape, dictating his reviews, and submitting them to the English teacher for comments, her reactions were overwhelmingly positive. She helped him transcribe some of his dictated book reviews and then printed them up and posted them in her room. Marty glowed with pride. His mood and actions at home reflected the glow: he actually talked about school and his day at the dinner table; he was able to listen to his brother and sister talk about their activities without mocking them sarcastically; he no longer had a fit when it was time to do his homework.

Help Your Children Resolve Problems with Their Friends

Lisa was driving to the grocery store with six-year-old Allison and her two-year-old brother, Max, in the backseat when she heard Max begin wailing because Allison had bopped him on the head with a book. In the parking lot Lisa comforted Max, reprimanded Allison, and then tried to figure out what had caused this burst of nastiness. After much questioning, Lisa learned that her daughter had a "problem at school." Her best friend, Rachel, wanted her to be in a "war" with the boys on the playground, the purpose of which seemed to be to stake out recess-time possession of the softball field. After reassuring herself that the war did not involve any actual fighting, Lisa asked Allison if she was still upset about Rachel when she hit her brother. When Allison said that she was, Lisa talked with her very seriously about what she might do to resolve the problem, told Allison that when she had a problem at school she should "talk to Mommy and Daddy about it," and reminded her that hitting her little brother was absolutely not permitted at any time for any reason. As the result of her mother's help, encouragement, and coaching, as well as a bit of role-playing, Allison called Rachel and told her that she wanted to be friends but that she could not be if she was going to be in a war. After Allison got off the phone with Rachel she was beaming with a new sense of self-confidence. She told her mother, "I'm really proud of how I handled that."

By taking her little girl's problem seriously, Lisa accomplished several things at once. She helped Allison resolve a problem so frustrating that she was uncharacteristically mean to her brother. She showed Allison that problems can be solved and that parents can help solve them. This, of course, increased Allison's willingness to ask her mother for help with other problems, a step that helped prevent future blowups with her brother. As the result of her mother's actions, Allison was encouraged to talk to her parents about problems with peers, she was taken seriously, and she felt very good about what she was able to do to resolve the problem. Finally, her parents helped Allison resolve a difficult interpersonal situation, teaching her that she could do the same in the future.

Tom and Diane Sanders asked me for help in reducing the conflict between their two girls, eight-year-old Debbie and six-and-a-half-year-old Jessica. When we met in March, Tom and Diane said that Debbie came home from school every day and "tromps on her little sister in every imaginable way." They explained that the problems had started in November and only worsened throughout the winter. They said that they had been putting off doing anything about it until Diane heard Jessica say to Debbie, "Why are you being so mean? You weren't mean to me last year." The cause of this truly nasty behavior was a mystery until we learned that Debbie had been teased herself by several of the class "leaders" for much of the school year. As soon as they learned of this, Debbie's parents spoke to both the school guidance counselor and the principal, who were distressed to learn that Debbie had been harassed in school but pleased that her parents had come to tell them about it. The principal spoke to Debbie's teacher, to the other girls' teachers, and to the playground monitors, emphasizing that it was crucially important that no child be made to feel uncomfortable in school. Debbie's parents told her what they had done and asked her to tell them and her teacher if the teasing happened again. That seemed to do the trick. Debbie quickly changed back to the truly delightful child and very considerate big sister she had been.

Take Your Children's Concerns Seriously

It is all too easy to dismiss children's conflicts and relationship challenges as "cute" or as "childhood spats," but they are extremely important to your children when they are going through them. If you doubt the importance of feeling rejected or just unpopular at school, imagine working with ten people and being convinced that six of them dislike you and the other four think you are a bore. Remember that your children's relationship conflicts are just as important and potentially distressing to them as yours are to you. When your children tell you about a problem with other children in school—and they will—be sure to respond specifically with advice on what to do to resolve the problem.

You may have been advised to be sympathetic—"It's sounds like that was very tough for you"—but sympathy will rarely be enough to change things for your child. What children need instead is guidance about what to do. Some parents tell me that they do not think they can give such advice because they had similar difficulties growing up. In fact, this is a plus: you know what it is like to have problems with other children, you can identify, sympathize, and remember how difficult it is. As an adult you have developed skills in dealing with the challenge of getting along with other people, and these skills can help your children with their problems. Skills you have used to handle disagreements with co-workers, negotiations with business partners, customers, or salespeople—all apply to these childhood conflicts.

You Don't Need a Ph.D. to Talk to Your Children

Here is a well-kept professional secret, previously the property of child psychologists and a few highly sensitive pediatricians. All you need do to understand your children's motivations better is to try to think like a child of his age. Don't worry about being wrong; your child will be glad to correct you if needed. In fact, being willing to guess about a child's motivation is probably the best way to overcome a child's (especially a very young child's) reticence. Parents are often concerned that they will get misleading responses if they use too many leading questions, that their children will "yes" everything just to be polite or "no" everything just to be difficult. If your child answers "yes" to some questions and "no" to others, however, this is probably not a problem. Another approach is to use a multiple-choice technique such as, "I can see that you are upset, but I can't tell if you're upset because you're tired, because you're not feeling well, or because you had a bad day in school." Try combining the multiple-choice technique with the "mind-reading" technique: "I remember when I was your age and was the last to be chosen for a team. It made me really sad and mad. I was mad all day in school and was still mad when I got home, and I think that's how you're feeling right now." As with the true-false and multiple-choice techniques, your child will tell you if you are wrong as long as you are willing and able to listen to her.

When your children answer your questions, listen attentively. Show them that you care and that you understand or are trying to understand what they are going through. Be prepared to ask enough questions so that you understand the nuances of the problems they are having, the fine points that can make the difference between really understanding and not quite understanding. You may begin to feel that you are interrogating your children, but if you are patient, ask your questions in a way that your children can understand, and explain that you are asking the questions so that you can help, your children will respond positively. Your efforts will be rewarded. It does make a difference whether your second grader is being teased by one child, two children, or six children. It does matter if the boy who made a joke about your son's weight is also a bit chubby, a good friend who mistakenly thought he was being funny, or the school bully.

If teasing or being excluded is the issue, try to find out how accurate your child's perception of the situation is, not whether she is being truthful, but whether she is seeing it accurately. So if your daughter tells you, "None of the girls like me anymore" or "Nobody chooses me for their team," try to find out if this is actually true. Talk to her teachers. Find out what happens at recess and at lunchtime. Children, like adults, are prone to making too much of negative experiences and forgetting to pay attention to positive ones, so they can remember every slight or insult with remarkable clarity but forget that they have many friends. To find out about the accuracy of what your child is telling you, first ask detailed questions such as "Are you the only girl who gets teased?" and "Do you mean that nobody at all will play with you?" and "Who are the girls who tease you?" These questions may annoy your child, but they will help you to help her through her problem by telling you if your child is in a truly horrible situation where literally every child in the classroom is nasty to her or whether it just feels that way.

When you have learned what is actually going on in school, sit down with your child and plan how to make things better. This is a challenging task that will require all of your creative and intellectual capabilities, so do not try to do it while watching television or reading the newspaper. Rather, take the problem as seriously as any other complex problem that presents itself in your life. Concentrate on finding practical solutions that fit your child's age.

Christine told her mother, Jessica, that she did not like being called up to the blackboard in her second-grade math class even though she liked math, because she was teased. "Edward always says, 'Chrissy is a dummy! Chrissy is so slow!' " Jessica took the problem very seriously and, after asking Christine about it, learned that Edward shouted out these comments in the middle of class, that it flustered Christine so much that she made errors and was embarrassed, and that the teacher had thus far done nothing to stop the teasing. Jessica recommended that the next time she was teased at the board, Christine should turn, face Edward directly, and say, "Edward Andersen! I am not a dummy. Your teasing hurts my feelings and makes it hard for me to do my work. Stop it right now!" Jessica answered Christine's questions about what the teacher might do (she thought this would put appropriate pressure on the teacher to do her job) and did a number of role-plays in which she and Christine took turns playing Edward and Christine. At the end of twenty minutes—that was all it took— Christine was much more comfortable with the prospect of being called to the board the next time. This is the kind of practical help that you can give your children when they are teased or made uncomfortable in some other way, whether at the blackboard, in the cafeteria, or on the playground. Do not worry about having exactly the right answer. Children's relationship problems, like those of their parents, always have more than one possible solution.

As children move into middle school, conflicts can become more serious. If, for example, your son tells you that he has been threatened with physical harm by another boy, the correct advice is to explain that this kind of behavior is not permitted in schools, that there are rules about this, and that he should unhesitatingly and unflinchingly report such threats to the appropriate school officials. Your child may be concerned about "tattling." You may be concerned that informing a school official of another child's bullying may just make it worse. Do not let these concerns stop you. Bullies prey on what they perceive as weakness and back off from any show of strength; a child who can enlist a parent and principal on his side has shown strength. For your child's sake, and also for the sake of other children in the school, it is of the greatest importance to stop bullying in its tracks.

Recognize Efforts to Be Helpful at Home

His parents were enchanted whenever eight-year-old Alex tried to teach four-year-old sister Amanda the words to a song or how to make the letters of her name, and they made sure that he knew how happy they were about his affection and his desire to help her. They told him how they felt; they took pictures of him helping Mandy, and they talked about his helpfulness to their friends within his earshot.

. . .

One of the most important ways that we can acknowledge each child, as meaningful as recognizing scholastic achievements, is by recognizing her unique contributions to the family. This is also one of the best ways to foster the growth of healthy self-esteem, a solid sense of self-worth, and cooperative and considerate family relationships. It can do as much to prevent really nasty sibling rivalry as it can to diminish that rivalry once it has started. All children with younger siblings are pleased when their efforts to help their parents and younger brothers and sisters are recognized. Of course, this assumes that they *are* making efforts to be helpful, a proposition that may raise some eyebrows. If we look closely, however, almost all children do try to show some kindness to their younger siblings. The efforts may be fleeting; they may be infrequent; they may not be the sorts of efforts that parents would choose—but they are efforts nonetheless. These small, tentative efforts to show kindness to younger brothers and sisters are best thought of as seeds—seeds that will need warmth and nurturing, a few words of praise, a bit of verbal Miracle-Gro, if they are to grow into trees capable of producing fruit on their own.

Small Efforts Are Important, Too

All of a young child's efforts to help may not actually *be* helpful: the efforts of very young children to be helpful often take forms that are not precisely in line with what parents regard as help. Five-year-old Ariel persistently asked to be allowed to help when her mother was diapering her eighteen-month-old brother. Her mother was well aware that allowing

Ariel to help would be sure to prolong the diapering process, a not totally welcome state of affairs. But she chose to let her help anyway, seeing it as a great opportunity to begin the sister-brother relationships in the best possible way. And she talked to her daughter about it as well: "You are such a great big sister, Ariel, and such a big help to Mommy, too." This may not seem like a great deal, but it did much to foster the affection between big sister and little brother, much to bolster Ariel's sense of self-worth, and much to inoculate against what easily could be a great deal of jealousy of a younger child and the attention he receives.

The Lack of Acknowledgment Hurts

I have often seen how failing to see a young child's efforts to be helpful can eat away at their small selves and how tiny changes in the ways parents respond to their young children can change the complexion of their world. I am thinking now of my work with Judy and Alec Bailey and their three children: Alec Jr., Barbara, and Jesse. Judy and Alec were very conservative people and extremely reserved in talking about what was really on their minds. They were in considerable distress about the frequent and intense conflicts among their children, as evidenced by their having sought my services, something that was clearly outside of what they would normally do. Judy and Alec were both quite honest about having grown up in emotionally repressed homes. Alec referred to his father's father as "a Prussian." Judy said, "We didn't talk about feelings in my family." I had great respect and admiration for Judy and Alec for having had the courage to involve themselves in therapy, given their backgrounds. My admiration grew when I learned that not a single one of their friends in their affluent and very conservative neighborhood had ever seen a psychologist, or at least no one had ever talked about it.

Our meetings tended to move slowly and to have many pregnant pauses. During one of these prolonged and awkward silences, six-year-old Jesse began talking about what she had done in kindergarten that day. Instead of thanking her for trying to help the conversation get going, her father told her to be quiet, that there were "important matters to discuss." It was obvious that her father's failure to see her efforts to contribute to the therapy process hurt Jesse. She stopped speaking and quietly curled up at the end of the sofa. Since I was certain Alec was committed to being the best parent he could, and that he would not knowingly hurt his child, I asked him if he thought it possible that she might have been trying to help ease the tension in the meeting rather than interrupt. To his great credit, he said, "Maybe that's so. She's a very sensitive kid." Even more to his credit, he grabbed the opportunity to acknowledge her efforts. In discussing this brief incident later, he said, "I never realized how such a little thing could help so much. After we left last time she was bubbly in a way she hasn't been for months."

Special Children Need Special Recognition

Children who have learning difficulties, developmental delays, and perceptual or physical disabilities are more like other children than they are different from them. This is nowhere more evident than in their need for acknowledgment of their attempts to be helpful to other people in their families. Andy, the youngest child in his family of five, was only three and a half and had come into the world under very difficult circumstances. As a result, he had a number of developmental problems, including delay in understanding speech and in speaking. At an age when most children are able to communicate their wishes and needs in language, Andy still relied on pointing and on often unintelligible noises to tell adults what he wanted. As a result, Andy was often frustrated, sometimes extremely so. At these times he lashed out at his mother and his sister. Although Andy tried to be helpful, he had to be corrected so often that these efforts in the positive direction were largely overlooked.

Based on a careful evaluation of Andy's abilities, we focused on acknowledging Andy's positive behaviors and on his willingness to follow simple instructions. When Andy complied with his mother's request to pick up a toy and put it in the toy box, she enthusiastically told him how pleased she was—"Good job picking up that truck, Andy! Thank you!"—and noticed that he was more and more willing to do what she asked. When he brought his jacket over so she could help him put it on, she was similarly enthusiastic. And when he did as she asked and gave his sister back her doll, she said, "That is really good sharing, Andy," and, turning to her husband, repeated, "Did you see how well Andy is sharing?!" Andy's parents found that the more they could make their requests easy to follow, the more Andy would follow them. So instead of asking him to gather up his socks, sneakers, and sweater, they asked him to do one thing at a time, praising him for each accomplishment.

The Value of Acknowledging Your Own Mistakes

Josh was the smallest and least athletic boy in seventh grade in his very competitive and sports-centered private school. He liked to read and was a serious student of magic, something that earned him the respect and admiration of many of his classmates. However, he was extremely sensitive about his size and lack of skill on the playing field, especially as compared with his younger brother. There were many days when his parents thought about taking him out of that school and having him attend the excellent local public school instead. Their reluctance to do so stemmed in part from their loyalty to the school—Josh's father and grandfather had both attended—and in part from Josh's connection to his friends there.

The situation was not helped by the history of athletic prominence in the family. Joshua Sr., Josh's grandfather, had captained three sports: his plaques and photographs were all over the athletic building. Josh's father, Josh Jr., set a still unbroken record in the freestyle and had received the sportsmanship medal at graduation. Josh's dad usually kept quiet about this, but he still felt uncomfortable and a little ashamed. He realized that he shouldn't and needn't feel this way, an insight to which his wife had contributed significantly. "I hate to admit it," he said, "but I feel embarrassed that Josh isn't a jock. I mean, up here I know it's not really all that important, but down here it sure as hell feels important." Unfortunately, his as yet unresolved conflict still emerged at times. For example, he sometimes let his disappointment show when Josh was not interested in going out for a team.

Sometimes the elder Josh's feelings were expressed in not

so funny humor. When Josh tripped over his book bag on the way to the bus one morning, he was devastated to hear his father laughing in the background. When things like this happened in the past, Josh usually found a way to get even with his brother for being the athlete and Dad's favorite. This time, though, Josh's father immediately realized what he had done and rushed to apologize. Josh not only felt much happier, he was much friendlier toward his brother later in the day.

No parent is perfect. Any parent may unintentionally do or say something that hurts her child. When this happens, face your child and let her know that you feel bad about what you did: apologize. Your child will see how much you care and will value your honesty and trustworthiness. Failing to apologize— or, even worse, refusing to apologize—will intensify the hurt and lead to anger and resentment.

The idea of apologizing to a child may strike some parents as unnecessary or even misguided. Bernard, a successful lawyer and the father of twelve-year-old Samantha and ten-year-old Matt, said, "In business we make mistakes every day, but we don't dwell on it, we just move ahead to the next project." Bernard was making a not uncommon mistake; he was bringing home not just the problems and stresses of business, but the ethics and attitudes of business as well. He was accustomed to "moving ahead to the next project" without stopping to repair the interpersonal damage that had been done as a result of a particularly heated exchange, a misread E-mail, or a negative performance evaluation. He got away with this at work because he was the boss. But he learned that this approach did not work at home. Each time he criticized his children unfairly, they drew away from him a bit more. When he learned to accept responsibility for having hurt them and for trying to make amends, they were relieved and appreciative.

Some parents believe that an apology is a sign of weakness. Others feel that apologizing will undermine their parental authority or water down respect. They could not be more wrong. Parents who have the courage to admit that they have been wrong are teaching their children that personal integrity is more important than always being right. A parent's apology also counteracts the resentment and anger that otherwise build up in children when they are unfairly blamed or criticized. And this resentment and anger is, of course, the force that impels many children to the kind of insensitivity and selfishness, the kind of truly nasty sibling rivalry, that parents find most distressing and upsetting.

Acknowledgment Reminders

Many parents are daunted by the task of increasing their awareness of the ways in which their young children are contributing, and trying to contribute, to family life. Most parents do appreciate their children, and most make the reasonable-seeming but incorrect assumption that their children are aware of this appreciation. I've prepared the following list of suggestions, not because I believe you do not sufficiently appreciate your children, but because you may benefit from reminding yourself of the specifics.

- *Before criticizing your child, ask yourself if she may have thought she was doing the right thing.* Take a lesson from Alec, the father of the kindergarten child who tried to ease the tense silence of a family therapy session. Consider carefully if your child's perspective on a situation may be so different from yours that what looks like a good idea to her seems different to you.

• *Make it a goal to find as many opportunities as possible to give credit to each of your children.* This is a New Year's resolution that you will actually be able to keep, since as soon as you start, your children's responses will be so powerful and will make you feel so good that you will never forget.

• *Never assume that your children know what you are thinking or feeling.* This may come as a shock, but your children do not know how much you love them, how proud you are of them, or how often you think about them and their welfare. I have seen many children act out, sometimes in some pretty unpleasant ways, all for the lack of a concrete statement or demonstration of affection.

• *Be positive.* Parents sometimes worry that too much praise is artificial, that it will water down real praise, and that it will undermine their children's capacities to make their own judgments. Phony praise is just that, phony. But praise for the positive aspect of an otherwise negative event, experience, or even behavior, if genuine, has considerable positive impact.

• *Give very specific advice to your children about how to resolve their conflicts with other children.* Remember how Lisa helped her daughter, Allison, resolve a conflict with her school friend by taking her concern seriously and problem solving with her, and do the same when your children bring home similar problems.

• *Be patient.* If your daughter is nine or ten, and if you have just begun to talk to her about her friendships and her concerns about those friendships, don't expect her to tell you everything all at once. The idea of your taking her concerns so seriously will be as new to her as it is to you. Given time, however, you'll both get used to this new way of talking and will both benefit from it.

• *Be consistent.* Children are geniuses at noticing what really matters. So if you tell your son that you want him to feel he can come to you at any time with any concern or problem, don't expect him to come back if you dismiss his worry about being teased at school as unimportant kid's stuff. Rather, take his concerns as seriously as your own.

• *Don't leave therapy to the therapists.* Try to think like a child. Be willing to guess about what your child is thinking and feeling, and be willing to be wrong. Ask questions.

• *Work with your child's teachers to find ways to give credit for efforts in school.* Talk to your child's teachers frequently. Find out what your child enjoys and what he avoids. Ask the teacher to help you identify your child's interests and strengths, and be ready to help the teachers do the same.

CHAPTER 5

How Does ADHD Affect Sibling Conflicts?

D ennis and Harriet Stevenson are far from the only parents to receive a teacher's note that reads, "Your child would do much better if he would sit still and pay attention, but he is constantly fidgeting and is distracted by the slightest thing." Many of these parents also hear, "Your child might have attention deficit hyperactivity disorder." Despite hundreds of magazine articles, dozens of books, and numerous television pieces, many parents are confused about what *attention deficit hyperactivity disorder (ADHD)* really is and especially about how it affects relationships with parents and siblings.

What Is Attention Deficit Hyperactivity Disorder, and What Makes It a Disorder?

All children younger than four are very active, and boys at this age are often extremely active. They all tend to be impulsive, and all young children lose interest in things more quickly than do older children or adults. All two-year-olds are in almost constant motion, and many three-year-olds, especially three-year-old boys, are equally active. This is the reason experienced professionals who evaluate and treat young children will not make a diagnosis of ADHD until a child is at least four years old.

Some children—most experts agree that the number is between 3 and 5 percent—continue to be much more impulsive and active than other children of the same developmental level even after the age of four. Other children continue to have great difficulty with what psychologists call the *modulation of attention*: they are unable to focus attention on the right thing at the right time. They often focus with great intensity on an exciting and favorite activity, then are unable to break off and move to something new. A child may intently watch his favorite television show or play his favorite video game for hours but be unable to shift his attention when his mother tells him it is time for dinner. This can cause problems, since it often looks as though a child is being disobedient when he literally did not hear what was said to him because his attention was so focused on the television or computer.

Attention deficit hyperactivity disorder is simply a term that has been adopted as a shorthand label: the diagnosis requires that a child be either much more inattentive than other children his age and developmental level or much more active and impulsive (hyperactive) than children his age and developmental level; that he show these behaviors in at least two settings, such as at school *and* at home; and that these behaviors interfere with his functioning in some meaningful and significant way. This last characteristic is especially important: a child who is restless and fidgety in class but is mastering material, earning good grades, making friends, and not getting into trouble should not be diagnosed with ADHD.

There are many problems with the diagnosis of ADHD. One is that attention deficit hyperactivity disorder sounds like an explanation, but it does not really explain anything: it is just a description. If a doctor tells you that your child is inattentive, overactive, and impulsive because he has ADHD, all he is saying is, "Your child is inattentive, overactive, and impulsive because he is inattentive, overactive, and impulsive." The second problem is that since so many young children are extremely active some of the time or in some situations, many of them are mistakenly diagnosed with ADHD based on their behavior in those situations without considering the extent to which their behavior is typical of their age.

This problem of overdiagnosis is exacerbated by the widespread use of psychostimulant medications such as Ritalin, Dexedrine, Adderall, and Cylert. These medications are so potent—they enhance the ability to pay attention in 50–75 percent of people (adults as well as children) who take them, and so safe—side effects are rare and usually reversible—that it is tempting for psychologists to recommend and for physicians to prescribe these medications as a "let's try it and see what happens" treatment. Many doctors who are normally conservative about prescribing medications will give Ritalin or Dexedrine a "trial" with a casualness they would never feel about a trial of an antidepressant like Prozac (although this is changing as well). If the medication works, it is then even more tempting to conclude that the child (or adult) "has" ADHD. But the medications have been shown to enhance attention even in people who clearly do not have ADHD. So if professionals forget that an accurate diagnosis requires that the child's ability to get along with other children, to succeed in school, or to function at home must be *impaired*, even more children will be mistakenly diagnosed. The result of all these pitfalls is a shocking pattern of overdiagnosis and overreliance on medications.

Many Reasons for Inattention

The diagnosis of attention deficit hyperactivity disorder is not particularly difficult, but it does take time: a careful evaluation requires two to three hours. When less time is available, as is always the case in the office of a busy pediatrician, other problems, especially school problems, can easily be mistaken for ADHD. One of the reasons for this is that many teachers have learned a bit, but not enough, about ADHD through their in-service training and in other ways. They have learned that some children who are distractible and restless have ADHD and that some of these distractible and restless children may benefit from medication, but few teachers have had the opportunity to learn how to differentiate between learning difficulties and attentional difficulties. If your child's teacher tells you that he appears distracted, restless, and unfocused, do not assume that he has attention deficit hyperactivity disorder or that he is lazy, but consider *all* the possibilities. For some children boredom is the cause: the work may be so easy that there is nothing for them to pay attention *to*. Another possibility is that your child's experience is like that of Tommy Richardson, whom I described in chapter 4: some of the work may just be too hard; it may lead your child to worry about whether he'll understand it and be able to do as well as both teachers and you want him to; and it may lead to a lot of anxiety, which of course can easily make a child fidget and look inattentive. I have seen many children whose teachers, like Tommy's, believed they had ADHD when they actually had very different kinds of learning difficulties. Children who have difficulties mastering specific kinds of schoolwork can easily behave in ways that make it look as though their problem is an inability to pay attention.

One way to experience this for yourself is to imagine that your boss or professional organization has required that you attend a six-hour seminar and that it is important that you master the material. Only when the first lecture begins do you discover that the entire seminar will be presented in Latin. Would you be restless? Would you fidget? Would you look and be inattentive? This is what it is like for children who are in classes that are pitched at too high a level, who have difficulty reading, and who have difficulty remembering what they hear, especially if many instructions are given at one time. Some of these children are like Tommy and struggle to keep up in most subjects; others are very quick in some areas but have a lot of difficulty in others, such as reading or math.

Real ADHD and Pseudo-ADHD

My remarks so far in this chapter may give you the impression that I do not believe *any* children have difficulties modulating attention, controlling their impulses, or sitting still, independent of learning difficulties. It may also appear that I do not believe that ADHD exists *at all* or that medication should *ever* be used. It is true that I am concerned about the pervasive overdiagnosis of ADHD and about overreliance on medication. It is also true that I find it helpful to consider children's behavioral difficulties as specifically as possible and not rush to connect them into a diagnosis prematurely. I think of two groups of children—the very large one so often mistakenly diagnosed and medicated, and the much smaller one with children who have genuine neurodevelopmental difficulties and require medication—as typifying pseudo-ADHD and real ADHD. Many children are restless or very active, act without thinking, or have difficulty paying attention to the teacher rather than to the activities outside the window. My preference is to help parents to find ways to address these as specific behavioral difficulties using specific behavioral techniques rather than medications.

However, I have also seen children who clearly did have genuine disorders and just as clearly needed some pharmacological help. Eleven-year-old Ricky was very bright, very talented, and very unhappy. He had literally no friends and was teased and scapegoated so badly at school that the guidance counselor called me one day in tears, asking for help. Things were no better at home. His parents were loving but had reached the limit of their patience. Ricky was not merely in constant motion: he had been in constant motion since birth. He had never slept through the night—it may sound impossible, but it was true. He never took a nap. He never sat through an entire dinner. His activity level and impulsivity had caused other problems as well. He was not what anyone would call a mean boy, but he had behaved with great meanness toward his six-year-old brother, Bruce. On more than one occasion he had impulsively and angrily done real physical damage to Bruce, the kind that led to trips to an emergency room.

After a comprehensive evaluation it was clear that Ricky had real ADHD. After this evaluation I recommended that Ricky begin to take Ritalin, not to make a diagnosis, but to help him to pay attention and to slow down. It helped him so much that six months later his father, a sociology professor who was initially strongly opposed to medication for his son, said, "A day without Ritalin is like a day without sunshine." Ricky had become a different child. He was much easier to be around; he had begun to make friends at school; he had totally stopped bullying his little brother.

Checklist for a Thorough and Expert Evaluation for ADHD

If you are thinking about having your child evaluated to see if he might have real ADHD, the following checklist may be helpful. A thorough and expert evaluation for ADHD will have the following characteristics:

• *The evaluation will be conducted by professionals who specialize in evaluating and treating children.* While some professionals who practice mostly with adults have obtained the training necessary to evaluate ADHD in children, it is best to arrange for an evaluation by a professional who specializes in evaluating and treating children who have behavioral and learning difficulties: child and pediatric psychologists, pediatric neuropsychologists, developmental and behavioral pediatricians, pediatric neurologists, and child psychiatrists. Look for professionals who are trained in and interested in behavioral as well as medical treatments for ADHD and who have a track record (your child's pediatrician can help with this) of being willing to consider other possibilities besides ADHD, such as developmental delay, auditory processing problems, reading problems, and other learning difficulties. Ask what percentage of the children they evaluate are found to have ADHD. An answer above 60 percent, with the exception of highly specialized pediatric settings, may suggest that the evaluators are not looking hard enough for other causes. Experts will be extremely reluctant to diagnose ADHD in any child younger than four.

• *The evaluation will take time.* An adequate evaluation will take at least two hours and may take up to three or four hours depending on the complexity of your child's difficulties.

• *The evaluation will use many kinds of information.* Look for an evaluation that asks you for and uses information about your child's medical and developmental history, his educational history, and your family history. Look for an evaluation that includes brief psychological testing of your child's intellectual potential and academic achievement (especially in reading), a review of school records, assessment of your child's behavior through the use of direct observation, a detailed interview with you and your child, and some form of behavior checklist or rating scale completed by you and by your child's teachers. In addition, many evaluators use a computerized assessment of concentration and attention and some add a brief physical examination. These are not necessary ingredients in every evaluation but can be helpful when other information is inconsistent or when a child has medical or developmental difficulties in addition to problems with attention and activity.

- *Medication will not be used as a diagnostic procedure.* Several decades ago many professionals believed that children with neurodevelopmentally based problems with activity and attention (those with real ADHD) had a "paradoxical" response to stimulant medications like Ritalin because they would seem to slow down when given stimulants. Children were given medication "trials," and if they responded well, the diagnosis was made. Now we know that children appear to slow down only because the medication stimulates the parts of the brain that aid concentration and attention and that a response to medication cannot be used to make a diagnosis because many children who do not have ADHD will also attend better if they take stimulants.

If one of your children tends to act without thinking, if she is much more active than other children, or if she has difficulty following instructions or listening carefully to what an adult or child is saying because she is not paying attention, there will be real effects on her self-esteem and relationships, as well as on you and your other children, whether your child has attention deficit hyperactivity disorder or not. ADHD does not cause sibling conflicts by itself, but all children who have behavioral difficulties like those I have just listed are more likely to have problems getting along with everybody—including, of course, their siblings. It is extraordinarily important to acquire the skills and develop the techniques that can help your children learn to follow instructions, to attend to what other people are saying, and to think before acting. There are several ways to learn these techniques. For many parents, books about children's behavior problems and what to do about them are a good place to start. Some of those with which I am familiar are listed in the back of this book. A second step, or one you may wish to take in conjunction with reading, is to consult your child's pediatrician for some specific behavioral guidance. If problems continue, you may wish to ask your pediatrician for a referral to a subspecialist, either for a diagnostic evaluation of the sort I discussed earlier or for therapy. The general consensus among professionals who treat children with these behavioral difficulties (impulsivity, inattention, high levels of activity, difficulty following instructions) is that psychologically based therapies that focus on helping parents learn specific behavioral techniques are most successful. I have included some guidelines about how to find and select the right professional for you in an appendix at the back of this book.

CHAPTER 6

Remember Whose Childhood It Is

Riding the train from his office overlooking Lake Michigan to his home in an exclusive North Shore community, Jason Waters thought about how far he had come and how far he still had to go. He grew up in Chicago, the fourth of five children of a hardworking but poor single mother. His clothes were all hand-me-downs; his possessions were few. He played sandlot ball with his friends but could not join an organized baseball team because there was no money for a glove or other equipment. Summer camp or swimming lessons were out of the question. Three decades later, as a successful insurance salesman living in that affluent suburb with his wife and two children, Jason found himself unable to spend money on what he regarded as frivolous activities.

His twelve-year-old son Jack's playmates were involved in the usual suburban round of swimming lessons, soccer camp, and basketball or hockey clinics. Jack often felt odd-man-out among his peers: he was not part of the group that went to swimming and sports clinics together and was left out of much of the sports-centered socializing so prominent among his classmates. Jason was completely unable to appreciate this. When Jack complained, his father's advice was typically, "Make do with what you have" or "I never had any swimming lessons when I was a kid, and I did fine." Jason tried to be a loving father, but his childhood hardships blinded him to his son's unhappiness. Jack had no way of knowing that his father was withholding certain activities because of his own deprivation decades earlier. Rather, he thought he had done something to anger his father or that his father simply did not love him as much as the other boys' fathers loved them. When Jack came home from school in a black mood because the other boys excluded him, his little sister was his first target: he teased her; he provoked her; he tormented her.

The Challenge of Seeing Our Children Clearly

Jason is not alone. Adults' difficult childhood experiences often continue to burn so brightly that they blind us to our children's unique personal and interpersonal needs. The way that this happens is at once obvious and profound. Everyone experiences some hurt, some loss, some disappointments in life, and one's own hurt, loss, and disappointment are always more vivid than anyone else's. When one's hurt or loss is especially severe, it may be impossible to see another person's difficulties at all. This kind of blindness can occur in the lives of even the most loving and caring parents and can make it impossible to see children's individual and developmental needs clearly. One of the most valuable things you can do for your children, and for yourself as well, is to try to overcome this limitation and increase your ability to see your children as they are, as unique human beings with unique personal, interpersonal, emotional, and developmental needs.

Jason's experience shows how difficult the challenge of seeing our children as they really are can be. Jason was neither selfish nor unfeeling. He loved his son and cared a great deal about his son's happiness. But when Jack asked to go to a sports camp, all Jason heard was his mother's biting response when as an eight-year-old he had asked for a baseball glove. The issue became so heated that it was still a hot topic nearly a week later when Jason and Maria came to see me. Jason just couldn't get away from the idea that he hadn't needed basketball camp and so Jack shouldn't, either. Jason was shocked to realize that the pain of a life that he thought was in the distant past could influence his relationship with his son so deeply and destructively. He wanted to find out why he continued to react so emotionally to his son's requests. He pushed himself to think about the difficult days of his childhood, remembered how sad and angry he was that his family was so poor, that he could not have what other boys could. At first he was overwhelmed by anger at his mother, but then he thought about what it must have been like for her to lose her husband just after the birth of their fifth child, to struggle to bring up three boys and two girls with no help from anyone else. He realized that she had done all she could for each of them and that she would certainly have bought him that glove if she could have. This new understanding helped him hear his son's requests in a new way. The monetary cost of granting Jack's request suddenly became much less important than the emotional and relationship costs of refusing to do so. Jack was accepted as one of the gang within weeks after he began to participate in activities. His incessant torturing of his little sister stopped overnight.

What can we learn from Jason's difficult experiences? First and perhaps most important is to remember that surprisingly strong emotional reactions do very often result from experiences in the distant past. Pay careful attention to these emotional signals. Try to see your reactions to your children's behavior objectively. Do you frequently find yourself yelling and threatening your children? Does your spouse or another family member tell you that you respond with intensity to your children without need? If so, take a moment to sit back and think carefully before you leap to defend yourself. Ask yourself, "Is this really worth getting so worked up about? Is my strong reaction really justified by the circumstances?" There are very few things a young child can do that actually *require* screaming and yelling in response. Except for potentially self-injurious behaviors such as stepping out into a busy road, there are perhaps no such activities. The next step is to figure out what triggered your anger. Here are some questions that may help you identify that trigger. Did something happen that brought back painful childhood memories? Did your child complain about something that you were not allowed to complain about when you were his age? Did your child, like Jack, ask for something you wanted but could not have at his age?

Just Because You Did It Too Doesn't Mean It's Not a Problem

Mitch was only six and a half when his parents first came to see me. Brenda and Jeffrey explained their request for help this way: "We're actually here only because his school made us. We know that there are some difficulties. We're not exactly happy that Mitch and his sister fight so much, and of course we can't approve of his getting into fights at school, but none of that would have brought us here on our own." Brenda's and Jeffrey's ideas about their son's behavior were different from what I was used to hearing. Jeffrey's was, "He's just being a boy. I was the same." Brenda added, "I had trouble making friends in elementary school, but things got better as I got older. I'm sure he'll grow out of it, too."

As we continued to talk, Brenda and Jeffrey reiterated that they were in my office against their wishes, adding that they were "very private people" and not comfortable talking about personal or family issues. I asked if they thought Mitch might be unhappy that the other children were beginning to avoid him, if they were concerned that if Mitch was aggressive at the age of six, he might become even more aggressive at the age of eight, ten, or twelve, and if they worried that Mitch might seriously hurt his younger sister if his aggression continued.

Then came the surprise. Brenda said, "Nobody ever took me to a psychologist when I was a kid, and I turned out okay."

"Do you think things would have been any different if your parents had taken you to a psychologist?" I asked.

After a long and awkward silence Brenda said, "Maybe it would have been different. I was not a very happy child, I'm afraid. I never really had a friend until I got to college. I actually was quite unhappy, I suppose." Then, reaching for a tissue, she added, "I'm really being very silly about this—it was all a very long time ago. And the important thing is that I was just as impetuous as Mitch, and I never hurt anybody. I don't see what everybody is so concerned about."

I felt then, and still do, that it was to Brenda's great credit that she was able to be so honest about her own experiences and feelings. This was also a necessary step for her in realizing that it was not only the school personnel who were unhappy; Mitch was extremely unhappy as well. Before Brenda was able to see and acknowledge her own past unhappiness, she saw so much of herself in Mitch that she was unable to help him. After making a courageous leap of faith, she was able to see that yes, Mitch was very much like her, but he needed help of a sort that she had never received. She was also finally able to recognize that while she had difficulty making friends when she was Mitch's age, and she occasionally spoke out of turn in school, she had never been even a tiny bit aggressive with either family members or schoolmates and that this was a huge difference, one that really did call for strong action. These realizations— neither came quickly or easily—that her son's difficulties were in fact not precisely the same as hers had been and that she would have benefited from professional help, freed Brenda to accept help for herself and for her son. We concentrated on helping Mitch learn to wait for his turn, to seek attention from adults appropriately, to modulate his responses to other children's comments, and to follow his parents' and teachers' instructions without his previous intense emotional reactions. Having cleared up some of her own baggage, Brenda was able to focus on her little boy's needs and provide the kind of firm and consistent guidelines and expectations that he needed. As a result of her hard work, and that of Jeffrey, Mitch quickly began to get along better in school and with his sister. Equally important, he started to feel better about himself as well.

The Past Is Always Present

Alan had many painful memories of his father comparing him unfavorably with his twelve-month-older brother. He remembered his father literally asking, "Why can't you be more like your brother?" The awful irony was that Alan and his brother could hardly have been more alike if they had been twins. Not only were they very close in age, they looked so much alike with their curly brown hair and deep blue eyes that they were often mistaken for twins. To make the story even worse, they shared many interests. Both were avid Red Sox fans, both listened to gospel music, both sang in the school chorus. They would undoubtedly have been close friends were it not for the competitive situations set up by their father. Alan had spent many years trying to understand what was behind the comparisons, to no avail. He spent just as many years resenting his brother.

When we met, Alan was the father of two boys himself: nine-year-old Christopher and seven-year-old Scott. Alan frequently talked with anyone who would listen about his lingering anger at his brother and at his parents for comparing him to his brother. His wife and friends all expected that Alan would want things to be different and better for his sons, and he did. But his own past colored his thinking and perceptions so much that his actions were often not consistent with his goals, sincere though they were. In his blindness to what he was doing and to what his sons were picking up from him—this was how he described it later—Alan was oblivious of what was going on.

One Sunday afternoon Alan witnessed a confrontation between his boys that made him feel he had not been doing as good a job of facilitating brotherly closeness as he had hoped—indeed, as he had believed. Chris and Scott were playing around in the backyard with a soccer ball. Scott was dribbling to get around his brother in order to score in the makeshift goal they had set up in the old swing set. As Scott approached, Alan saw Chris stick out a foot, tripping his younger brother, who fell, twisting his knee and cutting his leg quite badly on the garden sprinkler that the boys had used to mark the boundaries of their playing field. Alan's first reaction was to see if his little boy was okay and to comfort him. His wife heard Scott screaming and quickly came outside to see what was going on, and as soon as she did, Alan turned his attention to Chris: "What the hell do you think you're doing! You intentionally tripped your brother! Didn't you see where he was going!"

"He had it coming."

"What are you talking about, 'He had it coming'?!"

"He did. He said he was a better soccer player than me. So I showed him."

Alan's fury was such that he had to walk away, afraid that he would do real damage to Chris if he did not. As we began to work together and to discuss the many concerns that had been on his mind for years, Alan told me that the occurrences of that afternoon had been the catalyst for his seeking help. "I stood there and saw my brother and me thirty years ago. I don't want to repeat that pattern."

Alan was truly committed to helping his children develop a

friendship of the sort that he and his brother were never able to achieve. But even after considerable work, he often caught himself on the verge of praising one son at the expense of the other. At other times, such as when watching the boys playing a competitive sport, he stopped just short of fanning the flames of rivalrous competition. Alan was eventually able to bracket off his lingering anger at his brother and focus on helping his sons forge a lasting positive relationship. He saw how he could influence his boys positively, both by actively encouraging their cooperation and brotherhood and by refraining from contributing to intensely unhealthy kinds of competition.

A turning point came when Alan decided to reach out to his brother and try to rebuild a relationship with him. As Alan slowly became more comfortable with his relationship with his brother, he gained an even deeper appreciation of his sons' relationship and saw new opportunities to help his boys achieve the same thing for themselves. Now when he heard them arguing over who had won a game of Monopoly, he was quick to talk to them about the difference between a game and real life. When one of the boys mocked his brother after a particularly one-sided tennis match, Alan was quick to remind them that he admired both the boy who could win graciously and the boy who could lose graciously. Each day he found new ways to help his sons build mutual trust and respect where he had previously found it hard to do other than foster mean-spiritedness.

Childhood joys and fears alike affect all of our lives just as they did Alan's. It is natural to be especially sensitive to issues and experiences that hurt us as children and just as natural to be less aware of our children's needs in areas that reflect difficulties we had as children ourselves. But the more we can do this, the better we will be able to support our children's development. It is often worth tackling the very hard and sometimes upsetting task of revisiting and trying to sort out childhood hurts, not only for our own sake, but for our children's sake as well.

Greg and Eunice Jones originally sought my help because of the bickering among their four children, especially that between their oldest child, Guy, who was eleven, and the others. As soon as we met, however, it became clear that Greg had an additional concern. He was terribly worried that his son would never find his niche, that he would be so afraid of failure that he would never try anything new. "When I look at Guy," he said, "I see myself as a boy, and I want him to go for things the way I did. To tell you the truth, I was never a great athlete, but I always went out for the team, and I always made it because I believed in myself. It never even crossed my mind that I could fail. Even when I was in grad school—the first day my adviser told me that only one in three of us would make it all the way through. I remember saying, 'I know I'll be here. I wonder what the other two will be doing in a couple of years.' I want Guy to try new things. I want him to find out what he can do, and I don't want him to be afraid to fail. When I face a challenge I go in to it with the attitude that I'm going to win. Whether it's work or a golf game or anything else. And that's how I want Guy to feel."

Guy sat there listening to everything his father said as if in an especially dull social studies class. He looked blank, forcing a pleasant face, a hesitant smile on his lips. He looked so tentative, as if he were afraid to say the wrong thing, the thing that might disappoint his father. Guy thought his father a superhuman who never had doubts and never experienced failure. In Guy's mind there was no doubt that his father would be extremely unhappy and possibly angry if his son did not succeed in everything he tried. The solution was self-evident: if he tried only those activities in which he was certain of success, he would not need to worry about disappointing his dad.

Of course, Greg was not a superhuman or even a super-self-confident human. He experienced the normal range of doubts about his abilities and the normal range of anxieties about being successful. He had done well in his work life by working hard and by projecting an image of supreme self-confidence, despite his actual anxieties. This strategy did not work at home, however. Greg cared deeply about his son, but he was so preoccupied with continuing to convince himself that he was a "winner" that his advice to his son sounded like a motivational lecture or infomercial. He thought he was talking to his son, but he was actually talking to himself, trying to assuage his own insecurities. The effect was just the opposite of what he hoped for. His reflections on his past did not bolster Guy's willingness to face new challenges bravely. Rather, they convinced Guy that he could never meet his father's standards; they intimidated him, and they made him resentful of his younger siblings because they were not pressured in the way that he was.

The turnaround arrived only when Greg was able to be honest with himself: he did have doubts and worries, but he took on challenges anyway and often, but not always, succeeded. Once he had done this, it was not difficult to be equally honest with Guy. The result was genuine understanding and genuine support. Greg was surprised how his willingness to admit weakness helped his son to be stronger, but it did. Because he no longer feared his father's disapproval if his every effort did not meet with huge success, Guy was able to try things where success was not guaranteed. Sometimes he succeeded; sometimes he failed. His self-confidence increased, and his fear of failure decreased with each new challenge. The better he felt about himself, the less he resented his younger siblings and the less he bickered with them.

Your Children Can Get Along Better Than You and Your Siblings Did

Beatrice was tired of the constant squabbling between her two daughters, ten-year-old Emily and eight-year-old Robin. When we began to work together on this problem, Beatrice said that she and her younger sister, Jackie, were also two years apart and that they had not been, and were not, especially close, either. Beatrice said that it had never bothered her that Robin and Emily never played together or even talked to each other very much, but the fighting was more than she could tolerate.

Beatrice said that it never occurred to her that sisters could be anything other than polite strangers. She had been very close with her parents and with several friends she had known since they were in nursery school together, but never felt much intimacy with Jackie. She had never thought of closeness among siblings as a possibility and so had done nothing to promote it. The result was that there was none. Once Beatrice saw that there was a possibility of doing more than stopping the fighting, a possibility of helping her girls become friendly, if not friends, it was as if a long-shut window had been pried open. She looked for and found many opportunities to encourage her daughters to begin to build a relationship. She soon noticed signs of caring between them and was quick to point them out.

We can harm our children's relationships with each other by assuming that our own experiences with our siblings, both good and not so good, represent the only way that brothers and sisters can relate to each other. Parents who had disappointing, difficult, and hurtful relationships with brothers and sisters assume that this is inevitable and fail to see the potential for better relationships among their children, fail to see what they might do to help nurture those relationships, and fail to do so. But as we have seen, parents who do nothing to help their children get along more often than not end up with children who don't get along. Finally, parents whose closest family relationships were with parents and not with siblings may not even be aware of the possibility of closeness among brothers and sisters. Parents who had no real relationship with their siblings may not see this as desirable and may similarly do nothing to foster it even if it could easily exist.

Consider Your Parents' Humanity

All parents want to be better, more loving, more nurturing, and more helpful than their own parents were. This is a worthy goal and admirable. Yet comparing ourselves as parents to our own parents can be deeply troubling. Lingering resentments from childhood interfere with our abilities to see our children clearly, to appreciate their wishes, their hopes, their sensitivities, and what they need to develop into happy, healthy people.

Lingering resentments keep us trapped in and preoccupied by the past; they keep us focused on our own concerns and sensitivities; they interfere with our abilities to focus clearly on our children. It is unrealistic and unfair to expect young children to appreciate the personal, family, and societal stresses that affect adults' lives. But this kind of understanding of the previous generation is possible for adults.

It may never be possible to totally erase these resentments, but it is worth trying since it will directly improve our capacity to care for our children. One of the best ways to begin is to sort out our own feelings about our parents from the realities that defined their lives, including not just how their parents treated them but also how society and major world events treated them. If you are like most adults with whom I have talked about these issues, you will find that your feelings change after you learn what life was like for your parents during their childhood, adolescence, and early adulthood.

Suggestions for Talking to Your Parents

It sounds simple enough, learning what life was really like for your parents, but starting the conversation can be difficult and awkward. Think of things you can do to initiate such a conversation in a way that is comfortable for everyone, such as looking at the family photo album together, asking about what life was like when your parents were very young, talking about your grandparents, starting with a common experience like "It sure is a challenge raising children," finding out how they were affected by societal issues and world events such as pervasive racism and prejudice, the Great Depression, and World War II.

. . .

I hope that this chapter has helped you see how important it is to avoid the ever-present danger of projecting your own childhood wishes, hopes, fears, triumphs, and disappointments onto your children. Each of us is particularly sensitive in some areas of life. It is worth identifying these areas since they are the ones most likely to lead us to seeing our children as projected images of ourselves rather than as the unique people they are. It is equally worthwhile to identify our assumptions about sibling relationships, since these assumptions can powerfully affect how we see and respond to our children's interactions.

CHAPTER 7

When Children Try to Carry Parents' Baggage

Helping children learn to change their behavior is a difficult job and one that requires facing some difficult, even painful, truths. This chapter is about one of those truths: we parents are sometimes responsible for those aspects of our children's behavior that bother us the most. It is fashionable these days to encourage parents to give up their guilt. Experts tell us that genetics, birth order, and peer pressure conspire to undo the efforts of even the best of parents. We must not, we are told, blame ourselves or take on responsibility for our children's difficulties, whether emotional, behavioral, or interpersonal.

I agree that feeling guilty about things over which we had and have no control is both unnecessary and ill advised. When I counsel parents whose children came into the world with chronic illnesses such as sickle-cell disease or developmental disabilities such as cerebral palsy, I do everything I can to help them see that their children's difficulties are not the result of anything they did or failed to do. These illnesses and disabilities and many others like them are the result of unpreventable developmental accidents, often during the first weeks or months of pregnancy: they are the result of bad luck, not bad parenting.

When we move from the arena of developmental and medical difficulties to that of interpersonal difficulties and conflicts, however, the situation becomes very different. Children whose parents inadvertently burdened them with tasks, worries, and concerns that are more than they are prepared to handle often become angry, unpleasant, and uncooperative with their parents, their schoolmates, and their brothers and sisters. The same is true for children whose parents unleash frustrations and tensions from work or from adult relationships at home and on their children. In this chapter you will learn to recognize signs of this sort of burdening, how to come to grips with the possibility that you may have caused or contributed to it yourself, and what to do about it.

Jonathan and Kristin Washington's two daughters, eight-year-old Robin and ten-year-old Norrine, were extremely competitive. Kristin said, "They make everything into a competition, and not a very friendly one. When there's no real contest, they make one!" When there was nothing real about which to argue, they found something. Kristin once told me about a fall afternoon of leaf raking. Their yard was not especially large, but it did enjoy the shade of five very old and large maple trees that lined their street. When fall came, their yard was beautifully blanketed by the falling leaves. Kristin said, "There were leaves all over the place and extra rakes, but Robin and Norrine decided that they had to be in exactly the same spot, raking up exactly the same leaves with exactly the same rake, so a nice afternoon became a battleground."

We talked about some of the strategies you have read about in the first chapters of this book, such as acknowledging each girl's efforts, helping each identify her own strengths, and avoiding comparisons. Kristin and Jonathan agreed to try them. When we met again, however, they began by telling me that nothing had worked. After several minutes Kristin said that she had tried the strategies a couple of times and then dropped them. We talked more about the frequent conflicts between Robin and Norrine, and then Kristin said, "I'm supercompetitive myself, and I always have been. I was the same as a kid. It's probably why I've been successful at work. I can't stand to lose an argument, but I don't think I'm bringing it home to the kids."

Jonathan asked, "What about all the times that we get into it, you know, debating who should give the kids their bath, who should make dinner, whose fault it is that we're late for a movie?" Then he added, "I'm not saying that I'm perfect. I'm pretty driven, too."

Kristin was a forthright person and a very honest one. She soon realized that she had conflicted feelings about her children's squabbles. She really did dislike the constant bickering and intense competing. On the other hand, she also admired people, including her children, who were willing to be pushy to get what they wanted in life. These mixed emotions reflected her feeling about her own intensity and combativeness with so many other people, including her husband. It was Kristin herself who pointed this out: "I admit it. I sort of like being driven. I like the competition, I complain about it, but I've always been that way. It's who I am. There are times I wish I could let it go.

You know, just live without having to be charged up with my hand in the electrical outlet all the time. I worry that I'm doing the same thing to my children—encouraging them to be competitive without helping them learn that you don't have to compete all the time."

Kristin was right to worry. Available to me, but not to her, was the fact that she smiled and chuckled ever so slightly even while bemoaning her children's continuing conflicts and struggles. Kristin had discovered more than she realized about a major cause of her children's fighting. She was correct to worry about the possibility that she was somehow fueling her children's fighting, but she did not realize that each time she corrected one of her girls for being too pushy, she also smiled a bit and chuckled to herself as if she were amused. Once she was made aware of this she saw the connection immediately: "No wonder they don't listen to me when I tell them to stop fighting, if they think I think it's funny!"

Kristin said that she was not totally happy about her own way of relating to people but was still unconvinced that her girls were acting out her conflicts. She also said that she wanted to take a closer look at her own baggage. The process that resulted involved her learning more about herself and in being able to respond to her children's ultracompetitive behaviors in a much more helpful way. Instead of letting her pleasure that her children knew how to stand up for themselves become muddled with her distress over their fighting, she cleanly separated the two feelings. Now when her girls became nastily competitive or physically confrontational she spoke to them clearly, telling them that being assertive was a fine thing but aggression was not. She also made it clear that it pleased her when they were cooperative. They responded to this as she hoped they would. Neither girl became passive, one of Kristin's voiced fears, but they did become considerably more cooperative.

As the connection between her personal conflicts and her children's behavior became clear to Kristin, she took on the responsibility for resolving her conflicted feelings about her own competitiveness herself, rather than relying on her children to continue to draw her attention to the problem through their fighting. She became determined to be fully aware of everything she said and did that might make her children feel that she was amused or secretly pleased by their arguments, conflicts, and fights. She also started to think seriously about herself and how she related to people, including her husband. It took Kristin many months to sort out her personal concerns. Her children's behavior began to change much more quickly: the physical fights stopped; the arguing became less frequent.

The Challenge of Seeing Our Children for Who They Are

Understanding how parents who love their children become blind to their children's needs and difficulties can present a major challenge to anyone's understanding. No parent would knowingly encourage her children to argue and fight. No parent would intentionally rely on his child to soothe wounds accumulated in his own life. No parent would intentionally burden her child with concerns and worries that would be difficult for an adult to manage. All adults have experienced loss, pain, self-doubt, and rage at unfairness. The danger is that rather than facing the challenges inherent in trying to work through

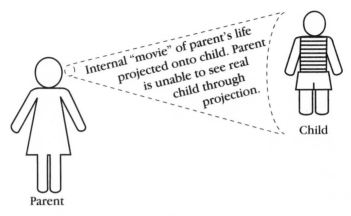

**Parent reacts to the projected "movie" image
not to the real child**

these issues from our past and present, we may find ourselves working them out through our children. Many of us run the risk of using our children to reduce our own anger, pain, grief, and feelings of inadequacy or loneliness.

It is natural to see ourselves in our children, but when taken to an extreme, when we fail to see our children clearly, instead projecting our own needs and experiences onto them as onto a movie screen, the cost can be overwhelming. Imagine a movie of your early life playing inside your head in an endless loop. Now imagine that this movie is being projected outside of you, onto a movie screen covering your child's face and body. Imagine that you are unable to see what your child is doing, unable to hear what she is saying, unable to see her facial expressions or appreciate how she is feeling, all because what would otherwise be a clear view of her is blocked by the projected movie. Finally, imagine that you respond to the projected movie images and sounds rather than to the real person who is your child. You would inevitably be angry when you should be sympathetic, critical when you should be supportive, blaming when you should be praising, amused when you should be stern, and oblivious when you should be delighted. This is what happens when you project your real or imagined self onto your child and then react to that projected child rather than your real child.

Parentification

If we cannot see our children's emotional, developmental, and interpersonal needs clearly, we will be unable to meet those needs. Rather, we may unintentionally push our children into meeting *our* emotional needs. Our children may be pushed into an almost parentlike role: they may become *parentified*. Some people believe that children become parentified when they are asked to fulfill roles often taken by parents. But a fourteen-year-old who is asked to watch a much younger brother or sister for an afternoon or evening is not being parentified. Rather, he is being given responsibilities appropriate to his age. The parentification that concerns us occurs when children are pushed into taking on parentlike roles, not in their relationships with their younger siblings, but in their relationships with their parents, so that they become parents to their *parents*. They are not free to be themselves but must be who their parents want them to be and must fulfill their parents' ambitions, often unmet expectations from *their* lives. Tommy Richardson's father's excited reaction that you first read in chapter 4—"No son of mine is average!"—is one example of how parents can easily fall into the trap of needing something so badly from their children that they fail to see who their children really are.

About ten years ago I was consulted by a very successful businessman who was concerned about his little boy's adjustment to kindergarten. His bigger concern, however, was that his son might fail to achieve, not just success, but fame and preeminence: "I don't want my son to grow up to be just another doctor, lawyer, or politician!" The burden that this five-year-old was being asked to carry was enormous, and it showed in his challenging behaviors at home, in school, and with his siblings.

Projections of Self-Criticism

Sharon, a thirty-seven-year-old single mother, continued to struggle with the low self-esteem that began early in her childhood. Even though she was very successful in her career, she still felt inadequate compared with her older sisters. She was plagued by thoughts that her sisters were more attractive, more intelligent, richer, and happily married. Sharon often told her friends that she found herself criticizing her ten-year-old daughter, Amanda, in ways that she never would do to Alex, her twelve-year-old son. Sharon nagged Amanda, a very pretty girl, about her weight. She commented ceaselessly about Amanda's taste in clothes, her choice of friends, and the music she enjoyed. Amanda resented this and felt that her mother unfairly preferred Alex. As a result, Amanda picked on Alex whenever she thought she could get away with it. Sharon was upset about this and yet unable to stop it.

At the suggestion of a friend, she decided to talk with a therapist about the increasing conflict between her children and about her own frustration and anger. As soon as she started talking about her children, however, she realized that she was just as upset about her relationship with her mother and sister as she was about her children's difficulties. When Sharon resolved her smoldering anger and resentment toward her parents through work with a therapist, her previously uncontrollable criticism of her own daughter simply disappeared.

Sharon remembered that her first reaction was, "I didn't know what I was doing. It never even occurred to me that I was talking to Amanda the way that my mother talked to me. Now I feel so guilty!" Sharon added that she quickly worked her way through this guilty stage, realizing that if she could change how she spoke to and responded to Amanda, she would have much less about which to feel guilty.

When You Need a Professional's Help

Sharon is not the only parent to feel the need of some professional assistance. Colleen and Brian had tried everything they could think of to ease the tension between ten-year-old Kelsey and her twelve-year-old brother, Christopher, but nothing seemed to work. When they discovered that Kelsey had begun to hide in her room so she wouldn't run into her brother and be teased or bullied, they decided it was time to get some outside help.

Six-year-old Dove's parents sought psychological help for a very different reason. Because of Dove's developmental delays, he was much less coordinated than his four-year-old brother, Paul. In addition, Dove tended to react somewhat impulsively when he was frustrated, which occurred often when he tried to do something that required physical coordination, such as riding a bicycle. Dove and Paul's parents were worried about the comparisons they anticipated would emerge and wanted to talk to an expert who was familiar with developmental disabilities and how they can affect sibling relationships. In other words, they wanted some consultation that would help them prevent sibling problems from arising, or at least would decrease their severity.

Forty-year-old Gerald, father of twelve-year-old Jeremy and ten-year-old Allison, looked back on his therapy and his journey as a parent: "I suppose I could have kept going the way I was. I don't think I was a bad father. But I was irritable and nasty, especially when I was under pressure or anxious at work, and I guess I just wanted to be able to look back ten years from now and feel good about how I was with my kids. I didn't want to regret my behavior."

In some families conflicts among siblings are so intense and have been going on for so long that they do not respond even to the most dedicated parents' efforts at changing them. Sibling problems may be compounded by the presence of children's or parents' emotional difficulties, such as depression or anxiety, other stresses on the family, or marital problems. A child's special developmental, medical, or educational needs may be both a source of stress on parents and call for special professional help. When these are the concerns, parents often look for a child psychologist or other professional with specific expertise in helping families with sibling and other relationship issues involving young children. The appendix contains some suggestions about how to identify possible professional help along with some suggestions for questions you may wish to ask to determine who will be best suited to help you.

When Personal Problems Are More Than Personal

Gloria and Mike's seven-year-old son, Nathan, and their ten-year-old daughter, Alicia, were the best of friends and the worst of enemies. Sometimes they played beautifully together for hours. All too often, however, they battled with extraordinary verbal and physical ferocity. Even when they were not battling, each child individually did much to upset Gloria and Mike, but especially Gloria, and especially when Mike was out of town on business or late getting home from the office. When he was home their antics were much more moderate, but when only their mother was there, things really got wild. Whether it was jumping on the furniture, spilling chocolate syrup on the living room carpet, or giving the dog an unneeded and messy bath, they seemed always to be into something, usually something that led to their mother becoming very upset and angry.

Gloria said, "Sometimes I get so upset about all the fighting that I just can't stand it!" She explained that there were times she cried for hours and sometimes could barely drag herself out of bed to face the day. Gloria also said that she'd had similar periods during which she cried a lot and had trouble getting going after the birth of each child, but she had not felt that way in years. It quickly became clear that Gloria was, and had been, quite depressed. She had thought of talking to her family doctor about some medication and about seeing a therapist but had done neither. When I asked if she thought her children were being affected by her depression, she said tearfully, "I know that they are, but I can't help it. I know I should be play-ing with them and helping them with their homework, but sometimes I'm just so worn out." Partially as the result of our talking about it, and partially as the result of having been so sad for so long, Gloria decided to go ahead with both her long-dormant ideas: therapy for support and for sorting out old issues and a visit to her family doctor to talk about safe medica-tions that might help her.

The combination of medical and psychological treatment turned out to be very helpful: Gloria's mood improved in about a month and, despite some ups and downs, remained much better than it had been for the past year. Surprisingly to her, the children's behavior improved as well. She and Mike had thought that her depression was brought on by the chil-dren's fighting: it was actually the other way round. Many of the children's upsetting behaviors, including the very violent fighting, were the result, not the cause, of her depression. They had been so distressed about her low moods and crying and so starved for attention that they had gone to any lengths to get her out of bed, even if it meant that they would be yelled at and punished. Once their mom was feeling better, none of this was necessary.

Trust, Trustworthiness, and the Exploitation of Trust

Children rely on their parents to make the world a safe and reliable place. Children whose parents provide this for them learn to trust the world and themselves, to trust that it is worth the effort to be kind to and considerate of other people.

Children who have been repeatedly injured in ways that damage their basic trust in the world, and especially in their parents, very quickly become angry, resentful, and unwilling—sometimes even unable—to do anything that shows caring or concern for other people.

When a Burden Is Shifted from Parents to Children

Elliot and Cindy Jobson came to see me about a number of concerns, but at the top of their list was the constant jockeying for position among their five children. Elliot said, "All I want is some peace and quiet when I get home, but what I get instead is squabbling and fighting from the minute I walk in the door. To tell you the truth, there are times I think about turning around and going back to work." Elliot was keenly aware of how *he* felt when he got home after a tough day at the office, but he was not particularly sensitive to how *his children* might be feeling about his anticipated arrival at home. When we began to talk about this, Elliot said that he very much wanted to know how his children viewed him and what their concerns were, even if they were not uniformly positive. When his children did not respond to his questions, Elliot complained that they did not communicate with him.

He was right, of course: his children did avoid talking to him directly when he asked them to, but not because they felt he did not care or because they feared his anger. Rather, they avoided any direct confrontation because they feared hurting his feelings. They saw how touchy he was about anything that led him to question his adequacy as a parent as revealed by the slight catch in his throat and the just perceptible moistening in his eyes when he spoke about his aspirations for his children and for himself as a parent. The reason for their nonresponsiveness was not immediately obvious, but the more Elliot talked about his desires to be a good parent and his fervent hope for his children's happiness, the clearer it became that he needed *them* to affirm his adequacy as a father and that he needed their approval so much that they dared not say anything at all negative to him.

Elliot wanted more closeness with his children and wanted them to talk to him about important issues. His intense need for their approval, however, combined with their feelings for him and for their mother, made them fear hurting him were they to speak the full truth: that he came home with so much bluster, it made them all anxious, and that in their anxiety they picked on each other. To his credit, Elliot was interested in learning about their perspectives and was willing to take the risk that he might not necessarily like what he heard; and in fact he did not. While it would have been unfair to ask the children to confront him with the truth, Elliot did respond to his wife's questions and to mine in ways that opened the door for his children to let him know how they had been feeling. It turned out that all of his children except the very youngest were both eager for his arrival at home in the evening and in a state of some agitation about it as well. What Elliot was not aware of was that he tended to open the door and bellow loudly about the first thing that displeased him. After he learned the truth, he tried to enter the front door in a calmer mood and with a less demanding disposition because he genuinely did care so much about them.

How Much Respect Is Enough?

Woody was ten years old when I met him, his parents, Margaret and Jack, and his twelve-year-old sister, Heather. Woody was basically a very nice boy but, as his parents accurately pointed out, he could manifest a striking lack of tolerance for other people's imperfections, especially those of his sister. This was not the first thing I noticed about the family, however. Rather, what impressed me was how incensed Jack was by what he referred to as Woody's "disrespect." I was at first more than a bit befuddled, since Woody sat quietly during our meeting, did not interrupt his parents when they were speaking, kept his sneakers off the furniture—not common in boys his age—and offered me a stick of his chewing gum.

As the meeting progressed, Jack said that he sometimes had to ask Woody twice to take out the trash, clear the table, or do his homework. To Jack these were clear signs of what he referred to as "disrespect." Jack found it intolerable because he felt it implied a lack of parental authority, something he believed was crucial to proper child rearing. So intolerable did he find these signs of what he believed to be disrespect that he responded with great ferocity to each instance. He was not content to remind Woody to do his chores. Neither did he find it sufficient to punish Woody for shirking the same. Instead Jack leapt on each transgression as an occasion to remind Woody of his basic inadequacy, of his temerity in speaking to adults the way that he did, of his essential lowliness in the family hierarchy. To Jack the unacceptability of his son's behavior was obvious: "If I ever dared to question my father the way he questions me, I'd have been on the floor in a heart-beat!" This revelation led to further discussions of what Jack's childhood was like. Jack's father was a retired career military officer who insisted on the kind of subservience and discipline that are stereotypically associated with the military. Jack's recollections of his father's style of discipline were striking: "I remember one time, all I did was say, 'I'll do it in a couple of minutes'—I don't even remember what I was supposed to do—and he busted my nose. Punched me right in the nose and broke it. My mother was crying. It was a mess."

Jack said that he had vowed he would never treat his children that way and was proud that he had not. Yet he still demanded the same kind of obedience that his father extracted from him. Was it any wonder that Woody welled up with anger and resentment or that he directed his fury in directions where it seemed relatively safe to do so—for example, toward his sister?

Over the course of a number of family meetings spread out over several months, I talked about these ideas with Jack, Margaret, and their children. Because they were parents who loved their children and wanted more than anything to do what was best for them, Jack and Margaret listened to my ideas with open minds. Not only that, they gradually changed their own perceptions and habitual modes of responding so that they were able to discriminate between noncompliance, which they met with fair but extremely firm discipline, and disrespect, which they no longer reported hearing at all. As we neared the end of our work together Jack said, "I used to think respect meant doing what I said when I said it. Now I think it means that when Woody is away at college and his buddies are talking about their fathers, he'll say, 'My old man is a great guy. I'd like to be just like him.' "

Parents often complain that their children do not respect them when what they mean is that their children do not do as they are told. A parent who regularly misinterprets any non-compliance as signifying disrespect will both experience and cause a great deal of unnecessary unhappiness. Adults who, like Jack, were raised in highly authoritarian households are often especially touchy about any possible challenge to their parental authority. They learned as very young children that their father's or mother's word was law and that any violation of that law would receive swift, if not necessarily just, punishment. Being squelched in this way produces intense anger in children, anger that lingers through adolescence into adulthood, often receiving its expression when one becomes a parent oneself.

Are You Burdening Your Children?
A Quick Checklist

Many parents place their children in positions of emotional caretaking without knowing it and certainly without wanting to. I hope this chapter has helped you to see that issues you may have thought of as affecting you alone are probably also affecting your children, especially in the ways that they relate to brothers and sisters as well. What follows is a list of so-called personal issues of this sort. I include it here not to raise feelings of guilt, but as a reminder that the more we can do to straighten out our own lives and to sort through our own baggage, the lighter the load will be for our children. If you answer "yes" to any of these questions, it is likely that you too have placed a burden on your children that only you can lift from them.

- Do you use alcohol or other substances habitually and frequently?

- Are you experiencing emotional problems such as anxiety or depression for which you have not received, but could receive, psychological or medical help?

- Do you yell at your children more often than you play with them?

- Do you blame your children more often than you praise them?

- Are you ever conscious of thinking of your parents or your own siblings at a time when you are upset with or angry at your children?

- Have you asked your young children to keep secrets to spare you embarrassment or worse?

CHAPTER 8

Family Loyalty and Loyalty Conflicts

Megan Simmons's twelve-year-old daughter, Tabatha, was always one of those children whom friends' parents adored. She worked hard in school, earned terrific grades, was active in Girl Scouts, played field hockey, had a very nice group of friends, and was able to talk to adults with both self-confidence and respect. Many of the parents of her friends would have been shocked to hear the way she talked about her ten-year-old brother, Connor: "He's so self-centered! I don't ever want to talk to him again! I wish I didn't have a brother!"

When Megan heard remarks like this one she always spoke to Tabatha firmly and with considerable feeling, for it upset her greatly: "I don't ever want to hear you talk that way about your brother again! We're a family, and I'll thank you to remember it!" Then, after she had calmed down, Megan usually spoke with Tabatha again: "I know you don't really feel that way. Down deep you love your brother. Just remember that words can hurt, and be careful what you say." But it continued to bother Megan, and not just a little. Her relationship with her own brother had been difficult when they were children and had remained strained at best: she fervently hoped that the brother-sister bond would be stronger for her children. Megan freely admitted that she still resented the "high-handed" manner in which Toby talked to her, that there were times she was furious with him.

Megan's husband, Colin, remarked on this one day when Megan was complaining about Tabatha's nastiness toward Connor: "You know, Megan, sometimes you talk about your brother that way, too; maybe that's where she gets it from." Megan was predictably miffed at Colin for pointing this out, but she quickly began to take seriously the possibility that he was right. It was true, she remembered, that she had been especially inflamed last week when Toby had called at the last minute to say that he would not be coming for Thanksgiving. What had she said? Something like "It's just like Toby to make a big deal about flying in for Thanksgiving and then to call the day before to say he had changed his plans, as if nobody else would be affected!"

When Megan characterized her brother as selfish, it seemed perfectly natural and ultimately true: he was selfish. But the word itself, "selfish," sounded so different when Tabatha used it to describe her brother. Megan was shocked to hear her words being used in this way: somehow they sounded more mean-spirited when coming from a child's mouth, and especially when directed toward her own son. She began to wonder, "How many other things has Tabatha copied from me that I didn't even know about?" From that time on Megan was much more careful about what she said about her brother. When she was upset with him she focused on the specific concern or specific behavior, rather than characterizing him as "selfish" or "self-centered." She talked to Tabatha about brother-sister relationships and explained that she actually cared a great deal about her brother and that was why she was hurt and disappointed when he did not come to visit. She told Tabatha that both she and Tabatha's dad hoped they could help Tabatha and her brother to have a much better relationship than Megan and her brother had.

As we have seen in earlier chapters, children are exquisitely sensitive to what we say and how we say it. They are also very interested in our family relationships, especially our relationships with our parents and brothers and sisters. Children pay close attention to how we get along with our brothers and sisters and to what we say about them. And what they see and hear affects them a lot, especially in the way they get along with their brothers and sisters. It is not unusual for children to model their relationships with their siblings on what they see in their parents' relationships with *their* siblings, or on what they believe about their parents' relationships with their siblings.

You need not have perfect relationships with your brothers and sisters for your children to get along. If you frequently speak ill of your siblings, however, your children will sooner or later incorporate these attitudes into their lives as well. They may be rude to their uncle or aunt. More likely they will begin to show the effects in their relationships with each other.

Very young children often imitate many things parents say and do without understanding what they are saying or doing. But a bigger problem, and a more significant cause of children's repetitions of what they hear, is that they have powerful feelings of loyalty to us. All children are naturally loyal to their parents: they just as naturally want to be able to express this loyalty by emulating and imitating us. How often do very young children say things like "I have a green shirt and Daddy has a green shirt"? How many children love or hate mushrooms depending on whether their parents love or hate mushrooms? That aspect of loyalty is perhaps one of its most obvious. One of the more subtle occurs when children emulate our relationships with parents and siblings, for better or worse. In chapter 6 you learned how a father's difficult relationship with his brother when they were children made it difficult for him to facilitate a caring relationship between his two sons because he unwittingly projected his residual anger at his brother onto one son and then the other. This is but one way in which parents' relationship with their siblings can contribute to sibling conflict among children. Another way is that the children themselves can, out of a feeling of loyalty, repeat their parents' patterns: "Mom never got along with her older brother, why do you expect me to get along with Jim?"

This aspect of loyalty can often be one of the more difficult connections to observe in our children, since it is the result of their having observed us over long periods of time and not simply a response to a single event. Because of this, and because we are not nearly as aware of how we sound as our children are, it often takes an outside observer to awaken us to what we are doing.

The need of our children to be loyal to us is very different from our loyalty to a favorite team, political party, or even to an old friend. All of those loyalties are chosen by us: we may feel tremendous conflict about the possibility of having to be disloyal to our close friend, political party, or favorite team, but we can choose to align ourselves with new and different friends, teams, or parties if we wish. If senators and congressmen can switch parties, we can, too. But our children cannot switch parents: they are stuck with us. And since they are stuck with us, the conflict they feel if faced with being disloyal is even more powerful. So is the pressure to be loyal, even in ways that neither they nor we are fully aware of. Loyalty conflicts are unavoidable for adults, but we can spare our children.

When twelve-year-old Angelique said, "Mom said that sometimes she thinks she should have stopped having children with me!" she revealed more than she knew about the root of her intense and often bitter struggle with her eight-year-old brother, Roy. When Angelique's mother, Meredith, said this to her daughter, she not only gave Angelique permission to be nasty to her brother, she *compelled* her to be nasty to him. In one sentence Meredith broke many of the rules described in earlier chapters in this book. She compared her two children; she focused on the negative; she failed to do anything to encourage caring and cooperation; she provided a model for competition and for treating one child as not quite a full member of the family.

Any of these errors by itself would have been enough to undermine a positive sibling relationship. What made it even worse was the strong bond between Angelique and Meredith. Angelique felt very loyal to her mother and usually found a way to put her feelings into action. One of these ways involved being especially nasty to her brother. The process by which this occurred was not mere imitation. Meredith's unthinking statement, almost certainly made in a moment of frustration, acted like a lever moving around a fixed point of Angelique's affection for and loyalty to her mother and prying Angelique away from any affection she felt for Roy. The strong bond of loyalty between mother and daughter also magnified the force of this unthinkingly harsh dismissal of Roy's value.

To be sure, Meredith may have had reasons for being frustrated with Roy, who was a very active and somewhat mischievous little boy. But as long as she blamed him for being himself instead of helping him to develop new ways of acting, his behaviors continued to irk, and his sister continued to blame him as well. When Meredith learned to appreciate him for who he was and to guide him toward the sort of behaviors she valued, mother and son got along much better and so did brother and sister.

Although Meredith's statement may shock, her experience holds an important lesson for all parents. Your children strive to be like you in as many ways as they can. It pays to be extraordinarily careful what you say to each of your children about their brothers and sisters. More than this, do not be surprised when one of your children picks on the very child who frustrates you the most. Rather, expect it. If you would prevent this kind of picking, look to yourself and to your attitudes about each of your children. You may love them all—in fact, almost certainly do love them all. Do you, however, *like* them all? Does one of them act in ways that bother you? If so, learn how to help that child behave more appropriately, follow instructions better, and be more cooperative. Help your child behave in ways that meet your expectations. Perhaps change your expectations. But do not expect your other children to treat that child with affection and kindness until you can do the same.

. . .

Tom Plumsee and his three brothers were always at each other's throats. Tom, being in the middle, had the brunt of it. His two older brothers, Geoff, who was thirteen, and Sam, who was almost twelve, were buddies. At six Jake was still the baby of the family. At eight and a half Tom felt too old to hang out with his mother and little Jake. Yet he was not welcomed by the older boys in their activities. Tom could be kind to his younger brother; he built Lego buildings with him, showed him how to kick a soccer ball, and sometimes read to him. He could also be cruel: he often called Jake a baby, teased him for sleeping with his stuffed dinosaur, and gloated about having a later bedtime. Phyllis Plumsee felt that something was very wrong and tried to talk with Tom about it. She asked him if he was having problems in school, if he was worried about his grades, if other kids were teasing him. But Phyllis did not really believe that these issues were causing Tom's unpleasantness. Rather, she was certain the true cause was that Tom's father, Frank, traveled so much for business and that he played with Tom very little even when he was at home. Beyond that, she found it hard to approve of much about the way Frank interacted with any of his sons. She believed that Frank was not a very good parent. She asked Tom often if he was angry that his father traveled so much. Frank saw the problem totally differently and was convinced that Tom was upset because his mother asked him too many questions, was "on him" too much.

Phyllis and Frank mistrusted each other in the critically important area of how best to respond to their children, and the children knew it. Their sons played one off against the other to get what they wanted, an inevitable consequence of having parents who did not see eye to eye. They also acted out their parents' mutual mistrust without knowing they were doing so. When Frank attempted to discipline Tom for entering his older brother's room without an invitation and "borrowing" some CDs, Tom said, "I know I shouldn't have, but I was so upset at Mom always being on my case." When Phyllis wanted to impose strict consequences on all the boys for fighting, Sam begged for mercy on the grounds that they were upset that their father was never around. These ploys, and others like them, worked on Phyllis and Frank because they played into the conflicts in their marriage. It was only after both realized that blaming each other for everything their sons did wrong was not helping anyone that they began in earnest to learn to parent as a team. Even after this important decision, they had to work hard to find new ways to make parenting decisions and to remember that it was in everyone's interests for them to stick up for each other. Phyllis began to tell her sons that their father was home as much as he could be and that he traveled only because his job required it. Frank told the boys that their mother was not "on their backs," but trying to help them grow up as they should. The result was not utopia, but it was a distinct lessening of tension among the boys and, of course, between Phyllis and Frank.

Everyone is by now aware of the terrible toll divided loyalties take on children whose parents are separated or divorced. What is less well known is the way children can be just as intensely torn between their mother's side and their father's side when parents live together but do not trust each other as partners or as parents.

Communicate Directly with Your Spouse

Some of these issues are subtle and can easily be missed, but it is often the more subtle loyalty issues that harm children the most. Adrienne Banks, who had promised to make cookies with her four-year-old daughter, Melissa, told her, "Daddy was supposed to clean the kitchen, but he didn't, so we can't make your cookies." Later that afternoon Melissa threw a doll directly at the head of her two-and-a-half-year-old brother, shouting, "You're bad!" Adrienne was totally perplexed by what may have precipitated this until her husband returned home from doing an errand and Melissa said to him, "You're bad, too!" When Adrienne asked Melissa why she had said that, Melissa responded, "Daddy is bad because he didn't clean the kitchen!" Although Adrienne initially felt better after venting some of her anger at her husband for not fulfilling his promise to do some kitchen cleanup, she was aghast when she realized how those few words had affected Melissa.

Shirley Templeton was very concerned about her husband's weight and high blood pressure. Frustrated by what she saw as his refusal to follow her requests and his internist's advice, she confronted him at the dinner table in the presence of their three young children: "If you don't care enough about the children to go on a diet, then be that way!" Two days later she overheard her eight-year-old daughter, Rebecca, plaintively ask, "Daddy, do you care about me?" It was then that she realized what she had done and vowed never to put her child in such an uncomfortable and painful position again.

. . .

All young children feel intense connections to both parents. When one parent "explains" the behavior of the other parent to children, as Shirley did, there is a clear risk that the child listener will feel pressured to side with one parent against the other. The parent who offers these critical "explanations" of the other parent's mistakes or failings is really saying, "Let me tell you something bad about a person whom you love very much." This is not a statement that can be easily ignored. Even children who are much too young to put such concerns into language are not too young to feel the tension and to respond to it: this is always terribly upsetting to them. The same is true when children are used in an argument between adults. In any family the temptations are great to have conversations and arguments that detour through the children. It may, in fact, be a familiar, even a natural, way to communicate for many parents. But it is not natural for your children. So when you find yourself disappointed in your spouse's behavior, tell him or her directly. Do not communicate through your children.

Mark Hampshire prided himself on how well he managed his children's behavior when they visited him on weekends and school holidays. The children, four-year-old Julie and two-and-a-half-year-old Jake, truly enjoyed their time with their father, and he was a very good parent. Not, however, a better parent than their mother, Eileen, from whom he had been divorced for nine months. If he believed he was a more competent and effective parent, and it often seemed that he did, it was because Eileen was always honest with him about the stresses of single parenthood and the difficulties of working full-time and caring for two young children by herself. When Mark heard Eileen complain about the difficulties of having two fussy children waiting for dinner, he felt superior: he had plenty of time to get dinner together before the children reached the stage of hunger-induced wildness. Of course, he had the advantage of not having responsibility for them on days that he worked, while Eileen put in a busy day before rushing frantically to the day care to pick them up each day.

Mark often told Eileen that he would like to help her learn to manage the children better. He wanted, he said, to share his knowledge with her. To Eileen, this offer seemed condescending at best. It seemed to her that Mark was not truly operating in good faith but was knowingly denigrating her adequacy as a mother. Mark insisted that he bore Eileen no ill will, that he did not want to criticize her, that he wanted only to help her to manage the children more smoothly. Although Mark may have believed this, the way in which he tried to help sounded more like a flaunting of his "superior parenting skill" than a generous offer of support. Jake and Julie heard many of these discussions, especially those that occurred when Mark picked up the children or brought them home after a visit. Jake was too young to understand many of the specific issues, but not too young to sense the tension. Julie, a very bright child, understood much more than either of her parents thought she could. The result of all this was that the children felt deeply anxious. They were far too young to be able to talk about their feelings—it is doubtful that this would have helped anyway—so they were left with no option but to act out their anxiety by way of tantrums and other disruptive behaviors. Because Julie absorbed more of the conflict, she naturally acted it out more as well, and much of that was unfortunately directed toward her little brother.

. . .

Children whose parents separate or divorce experience many difficulties, including the pain of intermittent separations from both the custodial and noncustodial parent, often cutoffs from extended family members, and disruptions in living situations. Children's strong loyalties also place them at risk for even more pain if parents put them in situations that require them to choose sides. Children who are explicitly or implicitly asked to care more about one parent, to love one parent more than the other, or to take one parent's side over the other feel great distress, distress that is inevitably apparent in their behavior.

Impossible Choices

Jonathan was fourteen; his sister, Wanda, was ten. Their parents divorced when they were eight and four. Since then the children divided their time between the two households—Sunday through Wednesday with their father, Thursday through Saturday with their mother. It was not a comfortable arrangement. The children's primary discomfort was not the moving back and forth, but the interrogations that followed. Each parent wanted to know what the children did at the other parent's home, and in some detail. It would have been bad enough if this were mere nosiness, but it was far worse: each wanted to be reassured that the children loved him or her more than the other.

The children were responsible for their parents' security: they had to behave parentally toward their parents, to nurture their parents, to reassure their parents, to be their parents' caretakers. The cost to these youngsters was immense. If they refused to answer the questions, they were disobedient to the questioner; if they did answer, they were disloyal to the other parent. Jonathan and Wanda loved their mother *and their* father; they were constantly pushed to choose between them.

Whatever "fairness" consists of, placing children in this kind of loyalty conflict is certainly an example of unfairness in the extreme. It is no wonder that Wednesdays, Thursdays, Saturdays, and Sundays were marked by bickering, arguments, and general unpleasantness of the sort typically labeled sibling rivalry. The root of this rivalry lay in the unfair bind imposed on Jonathan and Wanda, the requirement to choose between the two most important people in their lives.

When I first met George and Winifred their son, Colin, was six, their daughter, Nicole, was eight. Nicole and Colin were unhappy children. They were sad much more often than they were happy, grumpy much more often than they were pleasant, and oppositional much more often than they were cooperative. They bickered, teased, and fought much of the time when they were together. George and Winifred blamed each other for their children's behavior problems, and especially for their fighting. The nature of their blaming was especially hurtful. Winifred had been through a very rough period following the death of her mother four years earlier. Her family doctor had prescribed sedatives to help her sleep. Unknown to her, these powerful medications can be habit-forming, and she developed a strong dependency on them that eventually required intensive treatment.

Although Winifred had not taken so much as an aspirin for two years when I met them, George was vociferous in stating that all the children's problems began when his wife was "a drug addict." There was no evidence at all that this was true, yet George not only believed it, he harped on it with ferocious tenacity. There was no question that Winifred had been affected by the medications: she recognized that during the nine or ten months when her use of the medications, all of which had been prescribed by her personal physician, was heaviest she found it difficult to concentrate and tended to be forgetful, especially in the morning. But she had neither neglected her responsibility to care for the children nor been harsh or hurtful to them. The worst that could be said—and Winifred said it herself with considerable remorse—was that the medications probably dulled her sensitivity to her children's moods and needs during that period. The real damage to the children's functioning came later, when George criticized and blamed Winifred in their presence, making them feel they had to choose between their parents just as if George and Winifred had divorced and were fighting for custody of the children.

Loyalty in Blended Families, or, If I Like Dad's Wife's Children, Am I Rejecting Mom?

Nine-year-old Randy's parents had been divorced since he was six. When Randy was eight, Henry, his father, married Rosalyn and moved to a new home with her and her two sons, ten-year-old Mike and eight-year-old Christopher. Randy and Chris got along extremely well when they first met, when Henry and Rosalyn were dating casually. As the relationship between the adults grew more serious, however, the relationship between the boys became more difficult. At first Randy asked his dad frequently if he could sleep over at Chris's house.

Now that a shared house was a reality, however, Randy insisted on having his own room with a single bed, not the bunk beds he had asked for previously. He began to complain to his mother, Jean, that Chris was always bothering him, that Chris was "mean," and on occasion that Chris hurt him.

At first Jean took all these complaints at face value. She and Henry had agreed that whatever their differences, they would both put Randy's needs first, but she started to worry that it might not be a good idea for Randy to spend each weekend at Henry's home. She and Henry spoke about this and did their best to figure out what was causing the problem. It remained a mystery until one day when Randy, very angry and much less guarded than usual, blurted out, "It's not fair, you have everything and Mom is all alone!" When Henry tried to get Randy to talk about this he initially denied everything he had said. When Henry and Jean teamed up, though, they eventually wore his defenses down, and then Randy admitted that he did indeed worry about his mother being alone on weekends and that he did really feel it was unfair.

Knowing this, Jean was able to thank Randy for being so sensitive and so concerned about her and to reassure him that she was fine on her own for the weekend.

This is always a tricky issue. Caring parents do not want to endorse what appears to be, and is, a child's overconcern about a parent: they do not want to parentify their child by pushing him to worry about their emotional well-being; they do not want to do anything to encourage such overconcern once it has started. Many parents respond by telling their child something like "You just have a good time; don't worry about me." Sometimes such a message achieves the desired goal; often it does not, because the child continues to believe that he must care for his parent as Randy did; if he doesn't, who will? Because this sort of worry can be so persistent, I advise parents not to fight it, but to acknowledge it.

This was what Jean did. She told Randy how sweet and caring it was of him to be concerned about her. She thanked him for thinking of her. She told him how it made her feel good that he was so loyal to her. She acknowledged that it was true, that she did get a bit lonely when he was with his father. Then she told him that she felt this was something she needed to work on herself and that she was finding more and more things to do to make her weekends enjoyable. Most important, she told him that the one thing he could do that would really help would be to have fun during his visits, and especially to have fun with Chris. For many children in blended families this is the crux of the loyalty conflict. Getting along with their new stepsiblings involves more than working out a relationship with another child, more even than overcoming jealousy. They must be reassured that developing friendships with these children does not mean they are disloyal to their "real family."

Make Sure That Loyalty Remains a Positive Force in Your Children's Lives

Children's loyalty feelings and actions are overall positive: they are essential to children's connections to their parents and grandparents. As the stories in this chapter have shown, loyalty connections can also lead children to experience pain and to behave badly, especially with their siblings. Here are some things to bear in mind that will help you ensure that your children's loyalty to you remains positive for them and for you.

• When you have a disagreement with your husband or wife, speak to him or her directly about your concern. Do not detour through the children.

• Do not give in to the temptation to use your children as leverage to try to force your husband or wife into action to do something. If your wife consistently forgets to take her cholesterol medication, tape a note to the bathroom mirror or, if you are really desperate, talk to her physician. Do not confront her at the dinner table: "If you don't care enough about the children to take care of your health . . . !"

• Do not explain the action or inaction of your spouse or ex-spouse. This may seem benign but has the opposite effect.

• Remember that when your spouse suggests a different way of parenting, he or she is probably trying to help. Accept it and consider seriously that he or she may very well be right.

• Work to improve your relationship with your siblings.

• If you are divorced, encourage your children to enjoy their time with your ex-spouse. Do not put them in the middle.

CHAPTER 9

Facilitate Empathy and Altruism

What Is Empathy?

If there are ten babies in a hospital nursery and one of them starts to cry in distress because he is cold or hungry, many of the other babies will begin to cry as well. Walk through a crowded grocery store with an infant in your grocery cart. If your twelve-month-old laughs as you pass another parent with a baby, the other baby may very well begin to laugh as well. This is due neither to coincidence nor to gas or some other physiological process. These responses are the core of empathy, a baby's capacity to share another baby's feelings as if they were her own.

At dinner one evening four-year-old Matthew's parents asked about his day at nursery school and were surprised when he said, "Bad." When they asked why it was bad, Matthew said that Henry had chased Melissa and that Melissa cried. Matthew had experienced distress empathetically, not because of anything that he experienced directly, but because another child was upset.

This is but one way empathy can manifest itself in childhood, distress over the distress of another child. It also occurs when a young child experiences delight at another's pleasure. Empathic responses are not always negative. When three- and four-year-old children laugh with glee when one of their playmates smashes the piñata at a birthday party, they may well be empathetically experiencing the pleasure of the child who actually took the successful swing at that papier-mâché elephant or clown.

Empathy need not be restricted to childhood. Ideally the capacity for empathy continues through later childhood, through adolescence, and into adulthood. It always involves being able to understand how you might feel in another person's place, to experience the feeling even though you are not going through the experience yourself. When you gasp at another person's pain, become tearful at another's loss, or cheer another's success, you are probably empathically identifying with the other person's feelings. The same is true of your children.

We would all face a major hurdle if we had to teach children to be empathic in the same way that we teach them to read. Fortunately we do not have to do this because the capacity for empathy is inborn; this is why even two- and three-day-old babies respond as they do to the crying of other newborns. As parents, we need to foster our children's capacities for empathic responding and to be vigilant about not doing anything to impede it. Your efforts in this direction will receive ample reward: children who empathize with others follow an internalized Golden Rule; they automatically do unto others, siblings included, as they would have others do unto them.

Remember That What They See (and Hear) Is What You Get

Morgan was terribly upset at the way her eight-year-old daughter, Cheryl, was yelling at her five-year-old brother, Jeffrey, and let her know it: "Stop that screaming right this instant! I mean it!" Morgan was totally committed to teaching her children to care about other people and to show consideration in the way that they talked to each other. Her upset at Cheryl for yelling at Jeffrey was genuine and heartfelt, as was her shock when she returned to the kitchen and about five minutes later heard Cheryl berating her little brother: "Stop that right now! This instant! I mean it!" Cheryl talked with a close friend about this experience and found that her friend had had the same experience earlier in the week. She and her friend made a pact to stop screaming at their children and to use more positive techniques, such as acknowledging positive efforts and offering verbal and other forms of recognition instead. They agreed to offer each other support for doing so, a kind of informal support group. Each time they talked on the telephone or saw each other at the children's school, they reminded each other of the pact. The result was that over time—not all at once, but gradually—the children stopped yelling as well.

When Cheryl screamed at her children she showed them a way to respond *and* a way to feel. When she began to take a more positive approach, she showed them this as well. This kind of demonstration of how to behave and how to respond to other people, especially how to respond when you are unhappy or frustrated, is what psychologists call *modeling*, and it is one of the most powerful ways of influencing children's behavior. It is even more powerful than teaching because it goes on all day long; it immediately attracts your children's attention, and of course, one real-life demonstration is worth several thousand words. This does not mean that you should not talk to your children about being kind and considerate; you certainly should, and often. What it does mean is that you should not think that talking about kindness and consideration for others will do much by itself if your children do not have frequent opportunities to observe you *being* kind and considerate.

Choose the Right Models

Several years ago the Saybrooks consulted me about the very frequent physical fights among their three boys. Some of the fights sounded dramatic indeed. The description that stuck most vividly in my mind was one of their middle child, seven years old at the time, flying through the air feet first into the chest of his older brother. Near the end of an extended family interview, I asked how much television the boys were permitted to watch and what kind. When I heard that their favorite show featured superheroes who regularly and dramatically demonstrated their prowess with martial arts punches and kicks, including the very dramatic flying leap, the mystery about the flying attacks was solved. All the boys were much taken by the superheroes and tried their best to emulate them. The seven-year-old was not only the most influenced, but because he was temperamentally very active and a bit impulsive, he was even more prone to copy what he had seen on television. The modeling was more than he could resist, and of course, it was also totally unrealistic. On television shows like this one nobody is ever seriously hurt and nobody is ever particularly concerned about the possibility of injuring another person.

I made a number of suggestions to the family; the most pressing was to stop letting the boys watch this and similar shows that promote aggression. Since children in most households do watch hours and hours of television, it makes sense to monitor their television watching and to try to guide them toward programs that foster prosocial attitudes such as concern for others, cooperation, and generosity rather than antisocial attitudes such as violence and other forms of aggression. Many programs that appear on public television stations, those produced by the Children's Television Workshop and others, do foster the kinds of prosocial attitudes and behaviors you want to see your children exhibit. So encourage your children to watch television shows that demonstrate and foster cooperation, caring, and empathy rather than those that highlight aggression. Watch some of these television shows with your children and then talk to them about the values espoused in those shows.

Children who witness aggression, whether on television or in their homes, are very likely to imitate it. Modeling caring and consideration for others is by far the most potent tool that parents have for teaching their children to be empathic. Peers, television, and genetic predisposition play roles, too, but the single most important thing you can do if you want your children to learn how other people feel and to respond to them in caring ways is to model this yourself. "Do as I say, not as I do" simply does not work. Even the youngest children are acutely aware of how their parents resolve conflicts with each other, with their friends, and with children. Not only what is said, but how it is said, influences children profoundly.

Parents are often annoyed and frustrated by their children's yelling at each other, yet these same parents are frequently unaware of how often they yell themselves. If you are distressed by yelling among your children, listen to them carefully. Do you hear familiar phrases or familiar threats? If you do, and you probably will, do not waste time feeling guilty, but find a way to remind yourself to talk to your children in exactly the way that you would like them to speak to each other. If you don't want them to yell, stop yelling yourself.

Teach Your Children to Take Another Child's Perspective

Meredith often came home from school in an irritable mood and just as often spent the rest of the afternoon irritating her younger siblings. When Zandra, her mother, asked why she was so grumpy, Meredith often complained, "None of the other kids like me!" Zandra spoke to Meredith's teacher, who said that as far as she could tell Meredith was an accepted member of the group and was often sought after to participate in games.

. . .

Some children are social geniuses: they know intuitively just how other people are feeling, how other people feel about them, and how other people will react to them in different situations. Many other children, however, benefit from some direct help. If your child is one of the many in this latter group, take the time to talk to her about how she gets along with other children.

Perhaps your son or daughter is like Meredith in feeling that other children are teasing or rejecting when they are just having fun. If so, encourage your child to give others the benefit of the doubt. Help him to try on a different way of hearing other children's remarks and of responding to them. If he insists that his older brother calls him by a nickname in order to upset him, ask him, "When you call your friend by a nickname, are you trying to upset him or are you just being friendly?" When he responds that he would be using the nickname in a friendly way, but his brother would be using it in a mean way, challenge him. "How do you know that? What have you seen that makes you so sure?" Through questioning and sharing your experiences, you can help your child to see that he may be overreacting to his brother and possibly to other children as well.

When we talk about empathy we usually think of helping children to appreciate other children's sensitivities and other children's reactions to them. We focus on the effect that our children have on other children, both siblings and nonsiblings. We ask, "How do you think your little sister feels when you say that her dress is ugly?" or "How do you think your brother feels when you say that you don't want to play with him?" These are important questions; they help children become aware of how their actions can hurt their brothers or sisters; they provide the foundation for helping children learn to be more sensitive.

Eight-year-old Gregory Quince was terribly upset because his four-year-old brother, Zeke, imitated him. When Greg wanted to tell his parents about a song he had learned at school, Zeke wanted to sing it, too. When Greg wanted to lead the family in saying a blessing before dinner, Zeke wanted to do that, too. Greg complained, "He's always making fun of me! Make him stop!" Greg's anger and upset were totally unnecessary: Zeke was not teasing or mocking his brother; he was *emulating* him! When Greg's parents explained this, reminding him, "Imitation is the most sincere form of flattery," Greg was mollified.

Although this may seem to have little to do with empathy, it actually reflects empathy's other side. One way children can tell the difference between being teased and being admired is by empathically understanding how the other child is feeling. This kind of empathy helps a child understand what motivates another child. We do not usually think about this side of empathy, being able to intuitively understand what another person may be feeling that leads her to say or do something and being able to accurately judge another child's intent or motivation.

This is the aspect of empathy that both Meredith and Greg were lacking; it is an aspect of empathy that many children lack, and it is an aspect of empathy that can easily lead to much conflict and even to physical aggression among children, siblings and nonsiblings alike. Meredith's difficulties arose because she misperceived and misjudged other children's emotions and then reacted to what she thought other children were feeling

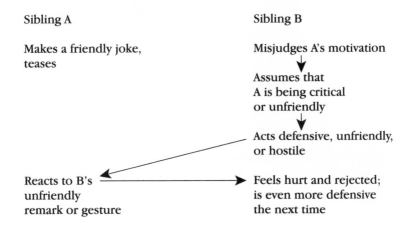

Sibling A

Makes a friendly joke, teases

Reacts to B's unfriendly remark or gesture

Sibling B

Misjudges A's motivation
↓
Assumes that A is being critical or unfriendly
↓
Acts defensive, unfriendly, or hostile

Feels hurt and rejected; is even more defensive the next time

rather than what they actually were feeling. This can be a problem for many children. A child misjudges another child's intent, whether that child is his brother or sister or an unrelated peer. After misjudging the other child's intentions, he then reacts as if his judgment were accurate. The result can be unpleasant in the extreme.

Recognize Empathy

Parents must make their values concrete and clear to children. This means learning to be generous and even effusive with praise whenever children spontaneously show their concerns and consideration for their brothers and sisters. The next chapter contains highly detailed and specific information about how to use both material rewards and verbal praise most effectively; the point here is that rewarding cooperative behavior, if done appropriately, will result in a marked increase in both cooperation and empathy.

Encourage Altruism

Four-year-old Matt makes drawings with crayons and on the computer for his older sister and puts them on her bulletin board when she is at school, "so she will think they are hers." Matt's empathic anticipation of his sister's response is not totally accurate: of course she will not think that she made the drawings. It is, however, altruistic: he gives her the drawings without any anticipation of personal gain. Very young children are frequently altruistic in this way. The challenge for parents is to find ways to nurture their altruistic tendencies and above all not to squelch them. When Matt's dog was very ill he placed some of his drawings near her bed to cheer her up. His mother told him that it was very thoughtful and sweet of him to do this and so provided the kind of acknowledgment of his generosity that is absolutely necessary to keep it flowing. Imagine how Matt would have felt if she had said something like "Don't be silly, dogs don't look at pictures"? He would probably have stopped giving his dog drawings, may well have been discouraged from making more pictures for his sister, and would have experienced a blow to his sense of himself as someone who is able to give meaningfully to other beings, human or canine.

Pets are extremely important to children, and a huge amount of modeling of both empathy and altruism takes place when children observe how their parents care for, or fail to care for, family pets. You may or may not think about your family dog or cat as a member of the family, but you can be sure that your children do. When our daughter was three she assured us all that Shana, our terrier-poodle mix, would surely learn to talk when she was a little older.

Five Ways to Enhance Empathy and Altruism

- Monitor your children's television viewing, and talk with them about what they see.
- Be conscious of yourself as a model.
- Encourage altruism with the family pet.
- Acknowledge and reward empathy and altruism.
- Do not tolerate aggression among your children.

CHAPTER 10

Bribery Is Okay

Seven-year-old Benjamin was having a difficult time adjusting to his role as a big brother. For the first five years of his life he was the "baby," the youngest of three children. At first Ben was excited about the prospect of being a big brother. He thoroughly enjoyed holding the new baby, feeding him a bottle, and helping his parents in various other ways. The trouble began when little Ronnie was two years old and began to be interested in Ben's toys and books. His parents tried to understand and to make allowances for Ben's need not to share everything, but they could not tolerate his pushing, shoving, and aggressively grabbing his brother.

The conflict grew so intense that Ben's parents decided to consult a child psychologist. At their first meeting the psychologist suggested that Ben's parents might use small rewards as a way of emphasizing how important it was to them that Ben be kind to his brother. Ben's mother was immediately interested in this suggestion, but his father was concerned that Ben would become so used to rewards that he would never learn to be considerate for its own sake: "I want Ben to grow up caring about other people without needing to get paid for it." The psychologist explained that the reward could (and should) be of very little monetary value but high emotional value: "Think of it as a concrete symbol of your caring rather than as payment."

Ben's parents and the psychologist talked about what the rewards should be and decided to use a combination of activities and material rewards. So when Ben let Ronnie hold his teddy bear before bedtime, his mother said, "Thank you for helping me with Ronnie. It's much easier to get him ready for bed when you let him hold your bear. Now I'll have time to play your new game with you before your bedtime, and if you can help again tomorrow, we can play another game or read stories." In order to lessen the conflicts that predictably occurred while dinner was being prepared, Ben's mother set up a chart on the refrigerator with a space for each day. She put a star on the chart just before dinner if Ben had been helpful while she was cooking. Ben was allowed to save up the stars to "cash in" for special desserts or small prizes such as a package of stickers or a small action figure. His mother realized that stars alone would not mean very much to Ben, so whenever she put up a star she made certain that she also praised Ben in a very specific and clear way. If Ben went to the living room to help Ron find a toy, his mother said, "That was great helping, Ben!" When Ben let Ron have a turn playing with his new truck, his mother said, "Great sharing, Ben. Thank you!"

What's Wrong with a Little Bribery among Friends?

Parents are sometimes reluctant to take advantage of this technique. Whenever I talk with groups of parents about using rewards for good behavior, at least one and often more parents are surprised, shocked, or angry, believing that their children should learn to do the right thing simply because it is the right thing, not to win approval, certainly not to win material rewards. Why should this be so? After all, adults' rewards are tied directly to their job performances. It makes just as much sense for parents to reward their children for good behavior.

When parents ask me, "Isn't offering a child a reward for good behavior tantamount to bribery?" I ask in return, "What's wrong with bribery if the result is good behavior, less conflict, and happier children and parents?" While for some people bribery may conjure up images of congressional or judicial influence peddling, what we are talking about here is encouraging children (through the use of verbal praise as well as physical rewards and activities) to follow instructions, to behave cooperatively, and to find appropriate and nonaggressive ways to resolve conflicts. Enticing a child to engage in behavior that will ultimately benefit him and other family members is very different from offering money to someone with the intention of getting them to break the law.

Another frequently voiced concern is, "If I reward my child for good behavior, won't she refuse to do anything without a reward?" This is, of course, a legitimate question, and it is possible that your child may become so "system savvy" that he will refuse to pick a pencil off the floor without payment. If rewards are used to highlight your caring for your child, not to substitute for it, you will have much less reason to be concerned about this sort of manipulation. Also, as you will see later in this chapter, the most potent rewards for cooperative behavior are verbal praise and recognition, not material gifts. These kinds of rewards have a very interesting and desirable effect: not only do they serve to encourage more good behavior and cooperation, they also become less necessary as your child gradually internalizes their messages into her own sense of self.

Some parents have difficulty giving serious consideration to rewarding those kinds of behaviors that they did naturally on their own when they were children or those things they were expected to do without either recognition or reward: "If I did what I was asked without any reward, why should my children need rewards?" The same is true in school. A parent who was a highly motivated student frequently cannot see the value or justification for offering even nominal payment for good grades, and the parent who was punished physically for being rude cannot fathom why any child should be rewarded for being polite. The biggest blocks to using bribery that I have encountered are those that arise from parents' preconceptions, preconceptions that in turn have arisen from their own experiences. If you wonder whether you may be experiencing preconceptions of this sort, you may wish to review chapter 7, especially the sections that talk about the ways that your own childhood experiences can limit and distort your perceptions of your children and their needs.

Don't Rewards Undermine a Child's Motivation?

Another concern voiced by many parents is that a child's natural tendency to be kind to others or to be considerate to brothers and sisters may be undermined by offering rewards. This is similar to the worry of parents and teachers that rewarding a child for good school performance may decrease her motivation to do well in that area as well. But clinical experience, bolstered by recent psychological research, has found that concerns about rewards undermining motivation have turned out to be false. As long as rewards are appropriate for the specific behavior or accomplishment and the child's age, the effects are usually very positive.

This research has shown that rewards have negative effects only when they are used improperly. When used properly, appropriate rewards actually enhance self-esteem, increase motivation for academic tasks, and facilitate greater family cooperation. There is no reason to let preconceptions or concerns that rewards will undermine your child's development interfere with appropriately reinforcing your children for the kinds of activities and behaviors you wish to encourage. Rewarding good or desired behavior is too powerful a way of teaching and influencing your children to be ignored. So the next question is: "What is an appropriate reward and how should it be used?"

How to Reward Cooperation Effectively

Mary and Dennis Seckel came to see me about six months ago because they were having great difficulty getting Evan, their six-year-old, to behave as they wanted him to. He rebelled at bathtime, had tantrums at bedtime, and acted as though taking turns when playing a game with his not quite five-year-old sister were a totally foreign idea. In getting to know them as a family, I asked what they had tried before and if any of those things had worked. Among the things they discussed with me was the suggestion of a friend to use a sticker chart. Their next remark was one I hear all the time from parents: "It worked great for the first two weeks, but now he doesn't seem to care."

Dennis and Mary told me how the whole family, including their two older children, participated in making the chart. Everyone was excited and enthusiastic, especially Evan, who had been allowed to choose some of the rewards he could earn for good behavior. They had a little ceremony when he earned his first sticker and another one when he cashed in his first ten stickers for a Beanie Baby. All of this occurred over a three-day weekend that coincided with the start of the sticker chart. When the work and school week started, there was not as much time for hoopla about earning stickers; neither was there time to take Evan shopping for the next Beanie Baby as soon as he had earned his ten stickers. A further complication was that Evan's older brother and sister began to complain that nobody made a big deal out of it when they picked up their rooms or brushed their teeth; certainly nobody took them shopping.

Over the course of three meetings we modified the reward system. Dennis and Mary kept the stickers but made sure that every sticker was accompanied by clear, specific, and meaningful verbal praise, such as "Great job picking up your toys!" They stocked up on the offered rewards so that Evan could receive his "reinforcer" as soon as he had earned it. And they reminded themselves that their older children deserved recognition for their contributions to the family, especially for their support of Evan's sticker system. They were too old for stickers or star charts themselves, but Dennis and Mary spent a full day with each of them as a way of showing how much they appreciated their efforts.

Many books for parents talk about rewards, often in the form of sticker or star charts, and suggest that they can be useful. Yet many parents who have read these books or been advised to "use rewards" experience frustration. Dennis and Mary's experience with their sticker chart is typical. Every week I meet parents who are concerned about their children's fighting, lack of cooperation, and refusal to follow instructions. Almost all of these families have tried some kind of sticker chart, and most of them tell me, "It worked great for the first two weeks, but now he doesn't seem to care."

Sticker charts are just one way of rewarding a child's good behavior. There is nothing magical about them; stickers and stars by themselves often do work extremely well for only about a week, maybe two weeks. Using rewards successfully to encourage and maintain the kind of behavior and cooperation you are looking for is not difficult, but it is a bit more complex than just handing out stickers. Using the right techniques, each of which has received a good bit of research, will lead to good results. The following pages contain answers to the questions I am often asked about how best to reinforce the kind of behavior you would like to see more frequently.

How Do Rewards Work?

Giving a child a *positive reinforcer* increases the probability that the child will be more likely to repeat whatever he did just before the reinforcer arrived. Children who are praised for taking turns when playing a board game are more likely to continue taking turns. An older sister who is praised for helping her little brother draw a dog is much more likely to want to help him draw a duck. A child who is acknowledged for helping a younger brother or sister solve a math problem or learn to shoot a basketball is much more likely to want to be helpful again.

A *negative reinforcer* also increases the probability that the behavior it follows will occur again, but it does so in a very different way: it reinforces by removing something unpleasant, not by adding something pleasant. A five-year-old boy hates bathtime. He screams and yells and is generally unpleasant as the appointed time approaches. His mother, exasperated, says, "I give up. We'll do your bath tomorrow." By removing an unpleasant event (the dreaded bath), this little boy's mom has negatively reinforced his screaming and yelling and carrying on. So negative reinforcement is a kind of reinforcement because your child will be more likely to do again whatever she was doing just before the negative reinforcement. The idea that it can be reinforcing for a child to be able to avoid something will be discussed more fully in the next chapter.

Differential reinforcement is a technical-sounding term for a simple and commonsensical notion. If we want our children to learn the difference between the behaviors we value and want to see more of and those we dislike and would prefer never to see again, we clearly must respond differently to these two kinds of behavior. In this chapter we will focus on what we can do to increase the behaviors we want to encourage; the next chapter will show you strategies and techniques for discouraging undesirable behavior.

In the previous nine chapters of this book, I have said quite a bit about the antecedents of sibling conflict, those experiences, attitudes, and events (such as being unfairly criticized or compared, having difficulties in school, being in loyalty binds) that often lead children to lash out against their brothers and sisters, to tease, to be supercompetitive, to resent, and to be hostile. I have also talked about what you can do to alter those antecedents in ways that sharply reduce the occurrences of mean-spiritedness among your children. Now we will look at how you can use consequences effectively.

How to Choose the Right Reward or Reinforcer

Thousands of research studies since the 1920s have demonstrated clearly that people of all ages (yes, adults, too) tend to do things that have previously led to desirable outcomes for them. We all tend to repeat behaviors that we believe will be followed by events that give us pleasure.

The most important rule for choosing the right reward is that it must be one your child values enough to change his behavior to earn it. Because we were all children once and because children of a certain age have a great deal in common, we can predict that some rewards will work for many children. As I am writing this the country is being swept by a Beanie Baby craze. There is no telling how long this will last, but as long as it does, the offer of a new Beanie Baby is a powerful reinforcer for most children between three and ten. Similarly, most children enjoy going to the local ice-cream shop; most enjoy being allowed to stay up half an hour later than usual; most enjoy watching their favorite video or television show. Beyond these few standard rewards, it is important to remember that our children's tastes and preferences are as unique as ours. Individually tailored rewards will always be the most effective. So to choose the most powerful rewards, think about your children's preferences and ask them to participate in the process. Remember that whether you think something should be a meaningful reward is unimportant; the important thing is that your child thinks it is worth earning.

Make Your Rewards Just Large Enough, but Not Too Large

This issue can make or break the success of bribery as a technique. The reward must be big enough to have some punch: if the reward you offer is too small, your child may not care enough to monitor or change her behavior in order to earn it. So do not expect much cooperation if you offer an ice-cream cone on Sunday as a reward for being cooperative and not fighting with siblings for an entire week. You will have much more success if the ice cream is offered for one entire day's good behavior. Too large a reward, on the other hand, brings its own problems. One major problem with too huge a reward is that your children may become satiated, thus no longer interested in future rewards. Staying with the ice-cream example for a moment, children who can earn "all the ice cream you can eat" on Monday are going to be less interested in being on their best behavior in order to earn ice cream on Tuesday. If your ten-year-old is rewarded for a week of cooperative behavior with a shopping spree at the local video game store, he will not be motivated to work for the same reward until he has become bored with the newly purchased games. If he knows that he will receive a new engine for his train set for Christmas regardless of his behavior, how likely is it that he will work to "earn" one through good behavior during November? If you want to motivate your eight-year-old daughter to be kind to her little brother, you may want to develop a star chart so that at the end of two months she can earn the American Girl doll she cherishes. If, however, she earns the doll after one day's good behavior or even one week's good behavior, she may be content and not want anything as much as she did the doll, may not want anything enough to work for it. Too large a reward can also easily distract both child and parent from the primary reason for bribery, emphasizing the importance of cooperative behavior. The best rewards are meaningful beyond their material value. A "big brother hat" or a "big sister jersey" means a great deal to a six- or seven-year-old older sibling; an afternoon's use of the family car can be a recognition of maturity for a sixteen-year-old.

Make Sure the Reward Is Achievable

We all have our own ideas about what we are likely to be able to achieve with some probability of success. The promise of a reward may increase our interest in taking on a challenge that seems achievable, but even the prospect of a very large reward is unlikely to influence our judgment about what is possible. Many people would be willing to walk a mile to earn $50 or walk five miles for $200. But fewer would want to run a marathon, even if the reward was $1,000, simply because most of us are not at all sure that we could finish a marathon. Fewer still would try to swim the English Channel for $5,000 or even $10,000. We would weigh the months of training, the physical effort, the cold water, the risk of being injured or drowning, and most of all the low likelihood of success against the very tempting reward and would say, "Thanks, but no thanks." We all make judgments about how likely it is that we will ever be able actually to gain the reward, and if the odds are too low, we will not try for it no matter how large the reward. How many people would attempt to climb Mount Everest in the winter alone for a $1 million reward? Probably someone would, but not very many. The same principle is important when setting behavioral goals and rewards for your children; reasonable goals and reasonable rewards work best. This is why the popular offer to take the children to Disney World if they behave well for six months rarely if ever works as hoped. The same is true for the trip that rewards good study habits for a semester.

Timing: When to Deliver the Reward

If you want your rewards and other reinforcers to have the maximum effect, be sure to deliver them right after the good behavior you are trying to promote. Every minute that passes between the child's cooperative behavior and receiving the reward will weaken its effect. And do not fail to keep a promise. If you rescind an offer of a reward, you will lose progress made in days, weeks, or even months. When you promise that trip to the corner ice-cream store if your children play well together until dinner, be sure to follow through, even if they battle during dinner. A deal is a deal, and they will not quickly forget a deal that goes bad. Just make a mental note to require good behavior both before and during dinner the next time.

In Praise of Praise

For many children praise is the most powerful reinforcer of all. Children are motivated to please parents, and appropriate verbal recognition of their efforts in this direction (in the form of accurate, specific, timely praise) can be very powerful. Praise is best used as recognition of specific behaviors: "You are playing so nicely together!" "I really like the way you let your sister hold your doll," and "Thank you for sharing your bedtime story with your brother." Specific praise can also go a long way to increasing your children's responsiveness to your requests and instructions: "Thank you for putting the napkins on the table," "Wow, you remembered to wash your hands before dinner without my even asking!" and "That's great the way that you hung up your coat."

Global praise such as "We love you so much!" or "You are so special!" is fine, but it provides neither the specificity nor the accuracy that is needed if praise is to be truly reinforcing to your child. There is also a risk that global praise of ability ("You are the smartest child in the world!") can lead not to increased self-confidence, but to its opposite. Children whose abilities are vaunted with global praise of this sort, whether it focuses on intellectual potential, athletic ability, or some other innate capacity, often become anxious rather than reassured. They may worry, "If Mom and Dad are convinced that I'm so smart, what do they expect of me? Will they be angry or upset if I am not the best in everything? Might it be better for me not to try things unless I'm sure that I'll succeed?"

How to Use a Star Chart

Star and sticker charts *can* be effective if they are used properly, but as Ben and Ronnie's parents learned, the chart by itself is not sufficient. To make it effective, combine the chart with the principles and techniques I have discussed so far in this chapter: put the star on the chart immediately after the good behavior; praise your child lavishly while you are putting up her star; make sure the rewards that your child can earn from stars are sufficiently interesting to him; use a menu of rewards that varies from week to week.

Notice When You Pay Attention to Your Children

The four of us were riding in the car when I noticed in the rearview mirror that our seven-year-old daughter, Ariel, and three-year-old son, Matthew, were singing songs together and having a wonderful time. I whispered to my wife, "Shhh, look in the mirror, but don't let them know you're looking. We don't want to spoil it." Of course, this was pure superstition; after we both told the children how happy we were that they were playing so well together, they continued to do so for the remainder of our trip. Yet how often are we parents influenced by just this sort of superstitiousness? How often do we choose not to attend to our children when they are playing cooperatively out of a superstitious worry that they will stop if we do so? And how many more times do we unconsciously ignore their cooperative behavior? In most families the answer is "Often."

Reminders and Guidelines

• Rewards are most effective when you use them to show your children how much you care about their behavior. They should reinforce, not replace, clear statements about what kind of behavior you expect and why it is important.

• Parents learn that a simple statement such as "It makes me so happy when you are nice to your sister; I want to find a way to help you remember to be nice, so we're going to have some rewards that you can earn for being good" can make the difference between a reward system that actually teaches cooperation from one that is viewed as a "system" to be beaten. "Look, if you can keep your hands off your sister for one solid day, I'll get you that toy you've been bugging me for," on the other hand, fails to put the reward in its proper emotional and interpersonal context. For some children it may even be taken as license to trip a sister and then claim, "You said to keep my hands off her."

• Bribes should follow, not precede, the behavior you want to see more of.

• Bribes are not just for sibling problems: the same reward and bribery techniques are useful in lots of other situations as well.

• Don't forget the praise. Remember that verbal praise and acknowledgment is often the most powerful reinforcer.

• Use a menu of rewards. Children can get bored, too. You would probably not return often to a restaurant that had only one item on its menu, and your children will not be enthusiastic about the possibility of earning only one type of reward.

• Don't be stingy with the praise and acknowledgment; you won't run out. Try the fifty-times-a-day technique described on page 25 in chapter 1.

CHAPTER 11

When Bribery Is Not Enough

As effective as praise and the use of material rewards can be in helping children learn to cooperate and get along together—and they can be extraordinarily effective—there will inevitably be times that you must discipline your children for inappropriate behavior, including behavior that may be harmful to other children or to adults. Taking on this responsibility is one of the ways that parents fulfill their obligation to help their children meet developmental challenges and develop the attitudes and habits that will enable them to get along with others for the rest of their lives. If we avoid this task, we ultimately parentify our children by leaving them to learn appropriate behavior on their own.

I have never met a parent who disagreed that it was important to teach children to refrain from aggression or that disciplining children is but one way of helping them to develop, yet I have met many parents who experience considerable difficulty in carrying out the actual business of disciplining. The difficulties are, of course, as varied as the families in which they occur, but a few generalities are possible. Harvey Jackson told me about the time he saw his ten-year-old son hitting his five-year-old: "I basically lost it. I screamed at Josh and called him an SOB. My wife said she was afraid I was going to get physical with him, that I was red in the face. . . . It took me hours to calm down, and then I must have apologized a dozen times. I still feel really bad about it."

This may strike some as extreme, but many parents become so angry when their children are aggressive with each other that *they* begin to lose control, sometimes becoming verbally or even physically aggressive themselves. Many more use disciplinary tactics that are ineffective, some of which can make matters worse. Other parents are upset by aggression among their children and are equally wary of becoming upset and screaming or hitting, as they were perhaps yelled at or hit when they were children. Such parents often feel that the best thing they can do is to leave the children to settle things on their own, to avoid getting involved. Finally, some parents believe that they should be able to reason with their children rationally: "Now, Jeremy, you know that hitting is not nice, and you shouldn't hit your little sister." On occasion this may be effective, but there are many more times when "Let us reason together" does not address the problem quickly or directly enough.

Parents experience two kinds of impediments to being effective disciplinarians. The first is lack of knowledge of how to discipline effectively and in ways that curb aggression and increase family closeness and enhance the parent-child bond. The second impediment is the constellation of feelings that parents experience when their children misbehave. Some parents, like Harvey Jackson, feel so angry that they have great difficulty calming down enough to be effective. Other parents may feel too sympathetic or worry that their child will dislike them. Knowledge of what to do and how to do it is necessary, of course, but it is not enough; all the knowledge in the world will not help parents who feel either too guilty to apply it or too angry to bracket off their own feelings long enough to do so calmly.

Four-and-a-half-year-old Terry frequently became frustrated and grabbed a toy from his six-year-old sister, Angelique. Sometimes he pushed, shoved, or punched her. Terry and Angelique's father worked very long hours and was often away from home: responsibility for much of the discipline fell on their mother, Carmella. She was frankly and honestly overwhelmed by the task of being a single parent, in fact if not in name. Carmella was a gentle person who found it easy to nurture her son but difficult to discipline him. Terry had been born with a cleft palate, and although Carmella had been told many times by different doctors that this was not due to anything she had done or failed to do, she continued to feel guilty about it. She also worried that Terry would feel bad about himself, so she tried to do everything she could to ensure that he felt loved. When Terry hit or pushed his sister she corrected him gently, "Now, Terry, you know you're not supposed to hit people." Terry often hit out of frustration; Carmella felt that she should comfort him, and she often did. Carmella and I talked about her longer-term goals for her son and about the benefits of correcting him more effectively for being aggressive. Carmella agreed that teaching him to behave appropriately would be in his best interest, even if it meant that she and he both might shed a few tears when she did it. She agreed that it was all right to discipline Terry firmly *now* in order to help him develop into a child who knows how to behave and how to control his frustration *later*.

When Sally Jamison heard little Natasha cry because her older sister, Lucretia, tried to yank the doll out of her hands, she ran to the living room to see what had happened. After comforting Natasha, their mother knelt down so that she was eye to eye with Lucretia. Then, using a very stern, intense, but controlled voice, she said, "Lucretia! No hitting!" She led Lucretia to a chair in the corner of the kitchen and told her to sit there for two minutes. After the two minutes were up she led Lucretia from the chair and said, "Lucretia, we do not hit people! Not ever!" Then she added, "It makes me very unhappy when you hit your sister because I love you both so much." Finally Sally gave her a big hug and told her again how much she loved her and how much she appreciated it when Lucretia played nicely with Natasha.

Aggression is a problem in many families with young children. It is both important and very possible to control this aggression effectively in youngsters. This is important because aggression can become a habitual way of solving problems, especially interpersonal problems, for many children. What is merely annoying or embarrassing in a four-year-old can easily become dangerous in a ten- or twelve-year-old. It is also important because children who respond to frustration with aggression will soon find themselves in a vicious cycle. Their aggression is quickly followed by the anger of teachers and parents; they become labeled as behavior problems; other children reject them; they develop chips on their shoulders and a feeling that others "have it coming" that they use to justify their aggression . . . and there you have it. It is possible because a great deal of psychological research and clinical practice has led to the development of effective techniques for controlling aggression that can be readily used by any parent.

Why Are Young Children Aggressive?

Aggression is a particular way to manifest anger, a way that involves verbal or physical assault directed toward another person instead of a statement such as "That makes me angry." The differences between aggression and assertiveness are profound, as I discussed in "Teach Your Children to Stand Up for Their Rights" on page 46 in chapter 2. There is a big difference between a child saying that he is disappointed, upset, or angry when things do not go his way and that same child hitting, pushing, biting, kicking, or throwing things. Children, like the rest of us, experience anger and frustration in response to all kinds of events and life stresses, many of which we have discussed earlier in this book. The ability to be aware of one's own anger and to express it appropriately is a sign of healthy development. But a child who reacts with aggression is showing signs of a failure to develop the kind of self-control necessary to getting along with her brothers and sisters, as well as with schoolmates.

Three-year-old Kenny Till usually got along well with his two older sisters and younger brother, but he could be quite disruptive and aggressive when he was upset. His mother described his outbursts this way: "He can be playing as nicely as can be until you say, 'No. You can't play with the light switch.' Or it might be, 'No, you can't watch television now!' Then he'll start throwing things or kicking or hitting or all three. The last time, he picked up his dump truck and threw it across the room at his sister. It nearly hit her in the head!"

Kenny's distraught mother responded to these incidents as would many loving parents: "I feel that he can't control himself, so I pick him up and hold him in my lap until he calms down. Sometimes I give him something he likes to eat to snack on, and usually after a few minutes he's okay."

"Are there other times when he acts up like this?" I asked.

"Usually only when he's frustrated. Like if I ask him to pick up his toys and he doesn't want to. Or if I ask him a question and he doesn't want to answer."

Mary Till did not realize it at the time, but her description of Kenny's temper tantrums and aggressive outbursts illustrated some of the things that contribute most to aggression in young children, especially in very young children. In trying to comfort him, she was actually rewarding him for bad behavior. When he acted up, even when he hit a sibling, she hugged him and gave him a sweet. He also was able to avoid activities that he disliked, such as picking up his toys. So whatever originally led him to be aggressive, it is no wonder that this kind of behavior continued. He gained attention and avoided having to do an unpleasant and difficult task.

It is important to make a distinction between the things that can cause a young child to be aggressive once and the things that cause the aggressive behavior to continue. Young children may become aggressive with siblings for many reasons. They may have been teased or ignored by a friend in school; they may be overtired or extremely hungry; they may simply want their sibling's toy or their parents' attention. There are, however, far fewer reasons why a child continues to be aggressive and why it may start to become a more and more frequent behavior: it may allow them to escape from an unpleasant, stressful, or difficult situation or task; it may lead to increased attention; it may allow them to possess something that they want (such as another child's toy).

If we want to understand what makes a child continue to be aggressive, we should look to what follows their aggressive outbursts as well as to what precedes them. Lucretia's aggression led to her getting control of the doll. In describing her difficulties with her son Kenny, Mary Till illustrated all three of the possibilities we looked at at the head of this chapter: Kenny avoids doing things he dislikes and finds difficult, he gains attention, and he receives material rewards in the form of snacks.

Time with and Time Away

The basic principle in disciplining any young child is to heighten the difference between the behaviors you wish to see more of and those you wish never to see again. This is the differential reinforcement you read about in chapter 10. So if you want to encourage cooperation and put a stop to aggression, you should be sure to praise cooperation in as effusive a manner as possible and with specificity, not just "What a good boy!" but "I'm so happy to see you sharing with your brother!"

When your child is aggressive, whether it is raising a fist in your face, taking a swing at another child, or even hurting another child, your response should be equally clear and specific. Disciplining a child for a raised fist may seem like an overreaction to some readers of this book; to others the connection between raising a fist defiantly to a parent may not be directly connected to this book's major thesis about sibling rivalry, but aggression is aggression and must be dealt with firmly.

Nearly every parenting book includes some discussion of "time-out," and nearly all parents have tried the technique, most with little success. The reason is simple: Few parents have received adequate information about what time-out (I prefer to think of it as time-away) really is or how to use it for maximum effectiveness to curb aggression and other undesirable behaviors. Time-away can be an effective and humane procedure for interrupting aggression among siblings if a few simple guidelines are kept in mind.

In using the time-away (or time-out) technique, keep in mind that time-away is neither a place (the "time-away chair," "Go into time-away") nor a means of reeducation ("Go sit on the foot of the stairs and think about how bad you were"). Neither is it intended to make your children suffer. Rather, it represents time away from the fun and time away from attention from parents; its purpose is not to make your children unhappy, but to help them learn that being aggressive will not lead to the goals they want, that it will not lead to more attention, to possession of their sibling's toy, to being allowed to watch more television, or to anything desirable. It is primarily a teaching technique, not a punishment technique. This is why I encourage parents to talk with their children about the need to have them spend "time away" from the rest of the family when they behave badly. This can heighten the distinction between fun time spent *with* their parents and siblings and time spent *away* from the fun.

Micah was playing in the large cardboard box that had contained the dump truck he received for his fourth birthday. Seven-year-old Rachel was calling him "dummy-head" and threatening to take the box away. Micah, who had a tough night with a stomachache, was beginning to cry. Rachel's father, George, looked at her and said quietly and calmly, "Time-out seven minutes." He took her to the landing between two flights of stairs, a spot where she could not participate in the activity in the family room and yet could be monitored easily. All she could see was the blank wall. She had no toys with her. She screamed and cried, lashed out with hands and feet, and threatened her father, "I'll kick you! You can't make me stay here! I'll put *you* in time-out!"

George avoided looking directly at his daughter. He did not respond to her taunts, and he carefully, gently, and firmly held her arms so that she could not scratch him during her temper tantrum. Rachel continued to struggle. She cried and screamed. She also tearfully accused her father of hurting her: "You hurt my neck! Mommy! Daddy hurt me on the neck!" George was glad that he had been so extraordinarily gentle in guiding her; if he had not, he would have worried that he *had* hurt her. After three or four minutes of sitting on the stairs, Rachel yelled out, "Only two more minutes! I've been here for five minutes already!" Her father did not look at her but said calmly and quietly, "It's still seven minutes, Rachel. The clock starts again every time you kick or hit." Rachel quieted down temporarily, but when George went up to check on her several minutes later she was in her bedroom, playing with her toys. Without a word he took her by the arm very gently and led her back to her spot on the stairway, noticing that she protested much less vehemently than she had just three minutes earlier. He left her there, went downstairs to play with Micah, and returned again two minutes later to see that she was once again in her bedroom. This time Rachel went even more easily to the stairway. When George returned for a final check, five minutes into the seven-minute time-out, Rachel was sitting quietly at the top of the stairs.

When the seven minutes was up, George came upstairs, said, "Rachel, seven minutes is up," and gave her a big hug. Then he talked to her seriously about why she had been put in time-out. "Rachel, you know Mommy and I love you very much." Rachel nodded. "And you know that even though it is very hard for us, it's part of our job to make sure you don't learn bad habits. Do you know what those bad habits are?"

Rachel responded immediately, "Like hitting my little brother or yelling at my little brother or taking things from him."

George said, "That's right," and gave her another big hug.

This incident illustrates a frequently occurring instance of conflict and aggression between young children and highlights how a parent can respond to these incidents in a way that quiets the immediate conflict, teaches self-control, and preserves respect and love between parents and their children. It is possible to do two things that you may have believed were mutually exclusive: value your child, help her to identify and verbalize her feelings; and exert control over her inappropriate behaviors while helping her learn to control those behaviors herself.

There are many points to notice in this story. The first is that Rachel's father, angry as he may have been, behaved calmly. He neither yelled at Rachel nor lectured her but simply escorted her to a place away from the focus of family activity. This is important, because if we wish to provide a meaningful consequence for undesirable behavior, we must recognize that much of the inappropriate behavior of young children is a way of seeking attention. So we must do all we can to assure that our efforts at discipline do not inadvertently give our children more attention in the process. Parents who are willing to take on the very demanding task of doing both these things at the same time (being very calm *and* very firm) show children how important they are, so important that parents are willing to take a firm stand even though it would be easier not to.

It is easy to become so excited while disciplining that our children will actually behave badly in order to receive the attention and excitement. The most effective way to prevent this is to remove the offending child from a place of excitement and fun to a place of boredom and to do it in as nonemotional a way as possible. It you are able to take your child by the hand or arm and lead him to a quiet and boring spot with a bored and disinterested look on your face, so much the better. If you can do all this without letting your child catch your eye, it will be better still. Rachel's father did not send her to her room, a typical parental response to children's bad behavior but a poor one since children's rooms are usually full of toys and games; being confined to one's room does not represent a negative consequence for aggression. Instead he chose a place for her to sit where he could observe her but from where she could not participate in the family's activities. George told Rachel to sit for seven minutes, following the widely accepted one-minute-per-year rule of thumb. He could have told her to sit for one minute and achieved much the same result.

Rachel's behavior became considerably worse before it got better: she yelled and screamed, kicked her feet, tried to hit her father, threatened him, and was generally rotten. This is something that you should expect, too. When you decide to adopt a new way of responding to your child's unacceptable behavior, you have made a major and serious decision. Your child, however, does not know this and is likely to regard it as a mere quirk, something you will get over if only she makes it difficult enough for you. She will want to see if you really mean it.

George did not take Rachel's behavior, threats, or insults personally. This may seem self-evident: why would any parent take the "I hate you!" from a young child personally? Yet when it happens it is easy to feel hurt, to respond as if such statements were genuine reflections of our child's feelings for us. George realized that were he to make the mistake of believing that his little girl truly hated him, he would be reacting as if she were an adult and not a seven-year-old and that he would be parentifying her as some of the children in chapter 7 were parentified. Taking her inappropriate behavior personally, and reacting personally to it would also have undermined his plan to ignore bad behavior while reinforcing good behavior.

If you want to make your use of time-away as effective as George's was, remember to be sure that your child has enough positive interaction with the rest of the family so that the time-away really represents a loss, be sure that you have the energy to stick with the time-away despite the inevitable flak from your child, be sure that you stay calm no matter how annoyed or angry you may feel, reinforce your child's good behavior when the time-away is completed, and lecture only once and after, not before, the time-away.

Choose Your Battles

If you would effectively discipline your children, decide what is truly important to you. If you attempt to impose discipline for matters that in the final analysis do not matter all that much, you will inevitably tire of the process, back down, and give in. The result will be that your children will not take the discipline seriously. It is not pleasant to see children teasing each other or making jokes at each other's expense. If you find this intolerable, if it is to you as inexcusable as physical aggression, and if you are willing to respond to each and every instance of teasing with the seriousness I have advised you to apply to physical aggression, then you may well be able to control it. But for most of us, it is difficult enough to be consistent in disciplining the really major infractions.

Not long ago a couple requested my consultation for help with the frequent conflicts among their three young children, some of which included aggressive outbursts. When the discussion turned to time-away the couple told me that they used a "time-out chair" when the children giggled too much at the table. Each household establishes its own rules, and one of theirs was that fooling around at dinner was not allowed. The problem with using time-out as a consequence for giggling was that neither parent felt strongly enough about it to follow through with their threats. Even very young children are well aware of the difference between the behaviors we find moderately annoying and those that we absolutely will not tolerate.

I remember well speaking with Betsy Wilbraham about her difficult time with her five-year-old son, Pete. The youngest of her three children, Pete was the only boy and by far the most stockily built, the most impulsive, and the most aggressive. He regularly hit his sisters and would not hesitate to kick or punch a baby-sitter or other adult who tried to control him when he was in the midst of a temper tantrum. A complete and accurate account of his infractions of house rules would fill a notebook. Yet—this was the most striking thing—Pete would never so much as talk back to his mother, who said, "He knows not to do that to me."

What had Ms. Wilbraham communicated to her little boy that made such a difference? Simply this: she would not tolerate even one instance of such behavior. She never warned him,

"The next time you . . ." She never threatened; he just knew. When he was aggressive with his siblings, however, she tended to give warnings because she always wondered if perhaps another child had provoked Pete. The solution we discussed was to develop a set of clear house rules, any deviation from which would never be tolerated, even if the other kid really did start it. For most parents I recommend that the list begin with "No hitting, kicking, pushing, or biting," followed by "No breaking things," and possibly "No screaming." Remember that any aggression is bad, not just between siblings. In order for children to learn that aggression is not an acceptable response to frustration and that it will never lead to a particularly desirable result, it is important to be completely consistent. When Betsy implemented such a set of rules and responded to any instance of aggression toward other children as she did when Pete threatened her, his behavior improved quickly.

What's Wrong with Physical Punishment?

The question of whether or not to use physical punishment is one that concerns many parents. Physical punishment for the behavioral transgressions of young children is like a powerful medication with many possible adverse reactions. There can be no doubt that physical punishment "works" in the sense that it does lead to a reduction in the behavior that it follows. Punishment also can have some undesirable side effects, just like a powerful drug. Children who frequently receive physical punishment may become more aggressive, especially if the parent who punishes is angry at the time the punishment is meted out, thus modeling aggression as a way to vent anger and frustration.

Stop! You May Actually Be Reinforcing Bad Behavior

This section is for all parents who have tried to use techniques of reinforcement and punishment and been frustrated because they have not worked very well, perhaps not at all. If you see yourselves in this category, don't despair. It is not your fault: much of what is written about these basic behavioral techniques is both inaccurate and misleading. Reinforcement is not something that can be specified ahead of time. If it were, we would be able to say that all children will eat their dinners in order to be able to have dessert, that any child would behave well in order not to be yelled at, threatened, or spanked. In fact, though, the only way to know if something is actually reinforcing to a child is to see what effect it has on the child's behavior. If your child responds to something you do or say by doing more of what he was doing before, then whatever you did is a reinforcer. If your child responds by doing less of what she was doing before, it is not.

A man I've known for years was telling me how he often comes home late from the office, greets his two young children warmly with hugs and kisses, and plops down on the sofa to read the newspaper or his mail, paying no further attention to his children. The children, who have not seen him all day, or perhaps for two days if he was out of town, become rambunctious and unruly. His wife says, "The kids were great until you got home," without rancor but not without an edge in her voice. What, he wanted to know, had he done wrong? Actually it was not what he had done, but what he had not done. He had forgotten to notice enough about his children's positive responses to his homecoming, leaving them no alternative but to compel him to notice their negative responses. His wife was right: the children were probably doing great until he got home.

As parents we all want our children to learn to behave appropriately and cooperatively, yet we undermine ourselves every day. We breathe a sigh of relief when our children are playing well together and hope that if we are quiet and do not say anything, they will continue to do so, giving us a moment or two of rest. Then when they get bored and begin to act up, we jump up and shout at them to stop. All this has the effect of encouraging disruptive, uncooperative, even aggressive behavior in our children.

When They Are Doing It for Attention

When we say, "They're doing it for attention," we don't think about what we're saying. If they really are doing it (teasing each other, running around wildly, jumping on the furniture) for attention, then what ought we logically to do to get them to stop? You may have tried raising your voice, rarely if ever with any success. Perhaps you have tried threats, sometimes with brief success but never with lasting success. You may have tried biting sarcasm with equally poor results.

Why do these approaches not work? Because they are based on an assumption that children should not do things to get attention or that they think they need more attention than they really do. But children *do* need our attention. More than that, they want it, and nothing we can do will diminish that want. Besides, even if we could diminish the want, we would not like the result one bit because the result would be children who are emotionally disconnected from us, children who are visitors in our homes rather than part of the family—not a good outcome.

Attention is like food, water, and air to young children; it is their currency, their money. So the notion of convincing, compelling, or coercing them to seek less attention is futile. What other choices are available to us? One very practical choice is to change the ways we respond to our children's different kinds of behaviors. The tired father we just read about was actually doing everything to encourage his children to be more wild and disobedient and nothing to encourage the kind of behavior he thought he wanted. When they were in a good mood, he was relieved to have some peace and quiet, so he did nothing. When they started to act up he took notice of them, he spoke to them, he yelled at them, and finally he rather ineffectually disciplined them. The problem the tired father had was that he assumed that since he does not like people yelling at him or being angry with him, his children would feel the same way. He may be right, but he forgot that his children were so eager for his attention that even though they did not enjoy his being angry, they would continue to do whatever was needed to get him to look at, notice, talk to, and react to them.

When bribery is not enough, remember to accompany discipline with instruction, as Sally Jamison did when she told Lucretia that she was not allowed to hit her sister. All children respond best to punishment that is accompanied by a simple, honest, and direct explanation. Take all instances of aggression seriously. Respond promptly and firmly to any behavior that violates other family members' rights. Much research shows that early and consistent discipline of this sort is the most effective way to curb children's aggression. Develop a short list of behaviors for which there will be zero tolerance in your family. Inform your children that they will go to time-away (or time-out) for violations of these rules. After this, do not give second chances or warnings. Rather, do as you have told your children you would. To make sure that time-away is maximally effective, be certain that it contrasts with the fun of time-with.

CHAPTER 12

Self-Esteem and Generosity: The Cure for Sibling Rivalry

Six-year-old Madeline prides herself on being her two-year-old brother Matt's big sister. She likes to bring him his teddy bear at bedtime; she loves helping her dad read Matt's bedtime story. Sometimes she goes too far and has to be reminded that she is not Matt's "boss," but she still feels good when her parents thank her for being so helpful. Fourteen-year-old Jim feels the same way about his ten-year-old brother: he keeps an eye on him after school, often makes him a snack, and tries to watch at least some of his Little League games. His parents both work long hours. They frequently tell Jim how much they appreciate his helping out in the afternoon before they get home, how proud they are that he is so responsible and mature. They also make sure that he has plenty of free time for his own activities and for spending with friends. Jim never feels overburdened by his responsibilities because they are balanced out by the acknowledgment he receives and by the considerable efforts his parents make to ensure that they do not ask too much of him.

Madeline and Jim enjoy helping their parents by helping their younger siblings and reap considerable benefits from it as well. Their parents give them generous amounts of credit for helping out; they receive and enjoy the appreciation of their attentions from their younger siblings, and their self-esteem grows from being able to contribute to their families. The result is a benign cycle, the reverse of the vicious cycle you read about in chapter 2. Children are given opportunities to be helpful to their siblings, and so to their families; they are fully acknowledged for these contributions; their self-esteem receives

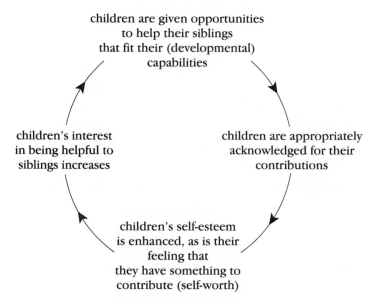

Benign Cycle of Self-Esteem, Acknowledgment, and Generosity

a boost from this, as does their belief that they have something important to contribute to other people; as a direct result, their interest in looking actively for additional opportunities to be helpful to their siblings (and to other people as well) increases.

It is, of course, important that the opportunities parents provide to children to give to others are consistent with their capabilities, both age related and those that reflect each child's unique strengths. Madeine's and Jim's experiences are illustrative. Both were given opportunities to do things for their younger siblings that were consistent with their developmental capabilities.

Most parents whom I meet, whether in the context of seeking counsel about how to help their children or as audience members at a talk for a group of parents, initially believe that all sibling conflicts arise from jealousy. As you have read, there are many causes for sibling conflicts. Some involve competition, and some reflect our own emotional and interpersonal issues as individuals, as parents, as spouses, even as children ourselves. There is no doubt that jealousy over attention from parents *can* also be a major cause of sibling conflicts. That is why it is so important not to compare your children and why it is so important to help each of your children learn about and develop his own unique talents and abilities. Although this connection between jealousy and sibling conflicts is evident, the opposite can be equally true. Children who are deprived of opportunities to contribute to their family often feel and show just as much anger and rivalry as those who are jealous of what appears to be favoritism for a brother or sister or the attention or praise that their brothers or sisters receive. Children who have too little opportunity to give something of personal value to their parents may be just as distressed as those who feel that they receive too little from their parents. When ten-year-old Barry complains that his five-year-old sister has an easier time because "all she has to do is be cute," he is not simply complaining that his little sister is favored. He is also complaining that it is easier for her to find ways to give to her parents, to give them reason to feel pride in their children and satisfaction in their own capacities to parent well. When Barry complains, he is not complaining that he does not receive enough affection; rather, he is complaining that he has too few opportunities to do things that cause his parents to swell with pride.

Spontaneous Giving

Anyone who has spent time in the presence of very young children has noticed their joy in giving spontaneously to others. They express affection and the need for affection by climbing into their parents' laps without inhibition. They take berries from their bowls and place them in their mother's or father's mouths or perhaps try to feed them to their plush animal toys. They freely and spontaneously kiss and hug their older brothers or sisters, their parents and grandparents; they crawl into any available and friendly lap. This spontaneity reflects children's basic trust that the world—and for the very young this means their parents—will treat them fairly. They trust that they will be taken care of, that they will not be hurt, and that their spontaneous affection will not be exploited. This trust allows them to be generous and to give of themselves as freely as they do.

Forced Giving

Madeline and Jim help their parents and younger siblings in ways that match their capabilities. At six Madeline is capable of helping with bedtime. At fourteen Jim is capable of watching his brother for a few hours. What about youngsters who are made to do so much that their own development suffers, to take on responsibilities that would tax much older people? Unlike Madeline and Jim, these youngsters are likely to resent both their parents and their siblings: they may keep their anger bottled up; they may voice it; they may even act it out.

Children and adolescents who are pushed beyond their years in this way are always acutely aware of the unfairness of their situations and of the lack of balance between what their parents do for them and what they are expected to do for their parents. There is nothing wrong with being asked to take out the trash, clear the table, or shovel the driveway. However, for children to worry about their parents' well-being when they are at school or to rush home from a friend's house so that their parent will not be alone is a very different matter.

Create Opportunities for Generosity
for Older Children, Too

Children naturally want to be helpful to and affectionate with their brothers and sisters as well as with their parents. Anyone questioning this need only observe how very young children follow their older siblings, imitating everything they do, asking when they will be home from school, insisting that they, not their parents, hold their hands when crossing the street, fix their breakfast, or give them their vitamins. As children grow, this aspect of their lives, like most others, becomes much more complicated. Self-consciousness interferes with the spontaneous displays of affection so common among the very young.

The need to show affection to parents and siblings remains, but the means to express that need are often absent. As boys reach the age of ten or eleven, for example, they often feel uncomfortable being physically affectionate with either parent or with their siblings. Youngsters who are deprived of opportunities to continue to be close with their parents and siblings may become isolated, angry, sad, even depressed. Parents who remain aware of the importance of helping their children identify ways to be affectionate, helpful, and nurturing can help children avoid this trap, one that becomes particularly problematic during adolescence.

Opening Doors for Children to Give

Rita Marshall's eight-year-old daughter, Victoria, asked if she could read a bedtime story to her four-year-old brother. Rita, tired after a long day and by her own description a bit grumpy, caught herself saying, "No, go to your room!" and then realized that she was about to lose two opportunities: to have a few minutes to herself and to let Victoria do something nice for her brother. She quickly reconsidered.

There is much that you can do to facilitate spontaneous giving among your children. The most important is not to say "no" too quickly when opportunities present themselves. If you observe your children carefully, such opportunities *will* present themselves more frequently than you might guess. You may hear your older child teaching your younger child a song or a knock-knock joke. You may catch a younger child offering an M&M's to his older sister. You may see one child making a drawing for another. Each of these chance observations can and should be an occasion for you to let both children, the giver and the receiver, know how pleased you are.

Generosity and Self-Esteem

All parents want their children to have high self-esteem, but a question that we ask too rarely is, "What kind of self-esteem do we want our children to have?" Although it is painful to think about, there are many people who feel very good about themselves while they are acting in ways that are harmful to other people. The movie *Wall Street* featured financier Gordon Gekko, with his message "Greed is good!" As played by Michael Douglas, Gekko had no problems with self-esteem whatever. Rather, he seemed to have a very full impression of himself and his self-worth, all the while flaunting the law, dismantling companies, and putting thousands of people out of work. It is possible to have high self-esteem and yet be selfish, self-centered, and greedy.

On the other hand, one can build up reserves of self-esteem and self-validation through making contributions to other people, both within and outside one's family. Clearly this is the kind of self-esteem we want for our children. We want them to have solid self-esteem, but not if it means harming or being insensitive to their brothers and sisters. Rather, we want our children to feel pride in their abilities to contribute to society, to care for others, including their brothers and sisters and those who are less fortunate than they. This is the sort of self-esteem that inoculates children against feelings of jealousy, envy, and resentment toward their siblings and other children as well. Children whose primary concern is to find ways that they can be kind and helpful to other people, as long as it does no harm to themselves, are much less likely to be touchy about real or imagined slights. They are free to enjoy another child's success rather than be threatened by it. They feel good when they can help a younger brother or sister learn how to play a new game or develop a skill rather than being worried that they will lose their special place in the family.

This has, of course, been one of the themes of this book: children whose parents create opportunities for them to contribute to the welfare of their siblings that fit their abilities, both developmental and individual; whose parents are able to recognize their unique strengths and interests, who are able to become clear enough in their own minds about their past difficulties that these do not distort their perceptions of their children, who are able to be nurturing enough so that children feel they have something to give to other people, especially to their parents and siblings, and who can avoid invidious comparisons that contribute to intense sibling jealousy—these children will enjoy being kind to, sensitive to, and considerate of their siblings' feelings and needs. They will also enjoy contributing to other people as they grow up and to society in general. These children have solid self-esteem and a positive evaluation of their value as people that both contributes to and reflects their capabilities to give to other people.

Looking to the Future

Gerry and his younger brother, Nate, are four years apart. From the time that Nate was born, their parents encouraged, supported, and reinforced cooperation, consideration, and caring between the two boys. As a result of their attention and hard work, the two boys got along extraordinarily well throughout their early childhood. As Gerry reached his teens, privacy became more important to him, as did his freedom to have time with his friends without Nate "tagging along." There were a few times when unfriendly words were exchanged, but those times were few and far apart. The two boys remained on generally good terms. They attended many of each other's sporting events and continued to enjoy fishing in the stream that ran back of their house. There is no doubt in my mind, or in the minds of their parents, that the years of closeness provided a cushion against the hard knocks that so often occur during adolescence. This book has focused on the problems and needs of younger children from early childhood through early to middle adolescence. But, as any parents of two or more teenagers will acknowledge, sibling issues continue and sometimes escalate during the turbulent adolescent years. By helping them to get along, and to overcome and move beyond sibling rivalry during their earlier years, you will do much to help your children prepare for the changes in their relationships as teenagers.

One of the greatest challenges of adolescence for parents and the adolescents themselves is that it is neither childhood nor adulthood. Parents feel reluctant to intervene too actively when adolescents have relationship difficulties; adolescents are reluctant, to say the least, to ask their parents for help with these same relationship difficulties in the way that they did during childhood. Adolescents strive for independence, and parents worry about fostering too much dependency. This would be fine were it not that your adolescents are not quite ready to handle *all* of their interpersonal difficulties without any help from you. They are no longer dependent as they were at the age of six or seven, nor were they as dependent at six or seven as they were at two or three. They may, however, still need your help from time to time just as they always have. The major difference, other than the complications of their lives, is that some care is required in how you go about offering to help, and even more care is required in how you go about asking if they need it. Adolescents do not like questions of any kind; they especially dislike questions about themselves and their current or recently past emotional states. It is a wise parent who recognizes this and acts accordingly.

If you are interested in finding out what is on your fifteen-year-old's mind, be prepared to wait, be prepared to listen, be prepared for silence. The greatest enemy of dialogue with many adolescents is the anxiety of parents. We are simply not used to asking a friend a question and waiting even one minute for a response. Neither do we have previous experiences with our children when they were younger that prepares us to wait while a fifteen- or sixteen-year-old thinks about whether or not she will respond at all, considers how she really does feel, wonders to herself if you could possibly understand the intricacies of her relationships, and finally weighs the possible benefits of sharing her thoughts and feelings against the risk of feeling misunderstood—or, even worse, of being on the receiving side of what sounds like yet another lecture.

All this takes time, so be sure to allow enough time for your conversation. Five minutes may have been plenty to find out about your six-year-old's day at school, but it will not be enough to find out what your adolescent's life is like. The first five or even ten minutes with your fifteen-year-old may be spent in silence, especially if it has been years since you had a real talk. Even if the matter is pressing, let your adolescent set the agenda. Sometimes an opening such as "I'd like to hear about . . ." or "I'm concerned that you and your sister don't seem to be getting along well," followed by "You don't have to say anything, just your listening is enough for me, but if you want to say anything, I'll listen and do my best to understand," is often helpful. The silence is not wasted time. It is as important as the words that follow and can do more to show your sincere interest than any amount of questioning. In fact, I advise parents of children between twelve and nineteen to do what they can to keep their questions to a minimum. Questions are great when your son or daughter is excited about an activity and wants to talk about it. They are not great, however, as a way to encourage a reticent adolescent to talk about his friends at school. The solution is to listen first, ask questions later, if at all.

Your Children Can Be Friends

People in close relationship inevitably have differing points of view, differing preferences, and thus disagreements. This is as true of our children as it is of ourselves. However, if you follow the guidelines in this book and put its suggestions to work for you, your children's fighting and arguing will decrease dramatically. For many parents this is an immediate goal, but not the only goal. Equally important to many parents is for children to continue to have close relationships with each other throughout their lives. A friend of mine said jokingly to her son, "You'll be glad that you have a sister when the time comes to put us in a nursing home." My friend is young and in excellent health. The prospect of being frail and in need of continuous care is far away indeed. Yet there is an element of truth in her statement to her son. Life presents may occasions, some joyous and some painful, when the support and comfort of one's brother or sister can mean a great deal. More than that, you will know that you have done as much as you can to ensure that your children will value and seek each other's company as they go through life, that they will care about and support each other into adulthood.

APPENDIX

Finding Psychological Help for Resolving Sibling Conflicts

Finding professional psychological help can be difficult. I offer this section as a guide through the sometimes confusing landscape of psychological services for children and families.

Making Sense of the Alphabet Soup

In most states the law restricts the right to use the title "psychologist" to those who have earned doctoral degrees (Ph.D., Psy.D., Ed.D.) in psychology. Some states also have provisions for limited licenses for master's-level (M.A., M.Ed., M.S.Ed.) psychologists, usually under the close supervision of doctoral-level psychologists. Before being licensed, a psychologist will have spent five or more years of graduate study developing expertise in psychological principles, techniques, and theories, conducting original research, and working with clients and patients under supervision. Training also includes a graduated series of practicum placements in hospitals, clinics, schools, mental health centers, college counseling centers, and outpatient clinics and a one-year advanced traineeship called an *"internship."*

Clinical child psychologists and *pediatric psychologists*, who specialize in working with children and their families, complete their internships in settings that serve children and families, such as child guidance clinics and children's hospitals, and have often completed one- or two-year postdoctoral fellowships as well.

Psychiatrists have graduated from medical school and earned either M.D. or D.O. degrees. Because medical training must prepare physicians for work in so many nonpsychological specialties, such as surgery and cardiology, very little time (usually only six weeks) is available for psychiatry education and training. After completing their undergraduate medical training, those who decide to specialize in psychiatry complete three-year residencies in general psychiatry at teaching hospitals, where they receive training and experience in diagnosing and treating mentally ill adults. Residents may also have the opportunity to do a one- or two-month rotation in a setting that serves children. *Child psychiatrists* go on to complete three-year fellowships in psychiatric or pediatric teaching hospitals, where they learn to evaluate and treat very seriously emotionally and behaviorally disturbed children and adolescents, generally with the use of medications.

In most states independent practice as a licensed or certified *clinical social worker* requires completion of a two- or three-year graduate program in social work that includes a one-year internship and leads to being awarded an M.S.W., M.S.S.S., or M.S.S.W. Licensed clinical social workers are identified by the LCSW or ACSW appended to their degree designations. Social workers who have acquired at least five years of clinical practice, of which at least two years must be supervised, may also hold the Diplomate in Clinical Social Work (DCSW). Social workers may or may not have experience in working with children depending on the settings in which they received their clinical training.

Marriage and family therapists graduate from programs that focus on family relationships and have earned either M.F.T. (master's of family therapy) or Ph.D. degrees. Their graduate work provides them with intensive knowledge of family dynamics and theories of family development and family therapy. Both master's and doctoral graduate programs in family therapy include a series of practicum placements. They may or may not include courses or training experiences in working with young children.

How to Find the Right Professional

There are a number of ways to identify a competent and helpful professional. Many people begin by asking a trusted relative, friend, rabbi, minister, priest, or physician for a referral. This is an excellent idea, especially if the person giving you the referral has actually consulted the professional herself. Professional organizations of psychologists, psychiatrists, and social workers located in every state and many major cities often have referral services that can direct you to qualified members of their profession. Telephone numbers and, where available, electronic addresses for some of these organizations are listed at the end of this appendix. You may also find it helpful to call one of the referral services that many large health care systems now offer. These services typically ask about your preferences and give you several choices, including information about each therapist's education, training, and areas of expertise.

Which Credentials Really Matter?

Sorting through the business of credentials can be one of the more confusing aspects of selecting a therapist. There are many, some are extremely important, many are less so. Some general guidelines may be useful. If you prefer a private practice setting, be sure to select a therapist who is licensed for independent practice in your state or one who is closely supervised in a way that meets your state's regulations. If you are unsure if a specific therapist is licensed, this information can be obtained from your state's licensing board for that profession.

If you choose a clinic affiliated with a university, hospital, or medical school, you may be given an appointment with a senior staff member (sometimes called an "attending") or with an advanced trainee working under close supervision. You may find it informative to inquire about the nature of this supervision and perhaps to obtain information about the trainee's supervisor. Training centers are typically eager to accommodate requests of this sort, as well as requests to meet the attending or supervisor.

Some Suggestions for Making a Selection

Whatever route you follow to locating potential therapists, there are several steps you can take to ensure that the person you choose is someone with whom you are comfortable, someone who understands the nature of your concerns, and someone who can help you to help your children get along better.

You may wish to prepare a short list of questions to ask the therapist when you call. The more specific your questions the better, because the therapist can then give you specific answers. So if you are looking for help in figuring out why you get so angry at your children despite your best efforts, you may wish to ask the therapist if she is familiar with this sort of problem, if she has training and experience in helping parents with their relationships with their children, and if she has sufficient background in child development to help you understand and respond to your child in more helpful ways. If you are seeking a therapist to help you apply the ideas and recommendations in this book, you may want to either ask the therapist if he is familiar with the book or briefly describe some of the techniques and concepts that seem especially relevant to your children and your family.

These questions should take no more than ten minutes, time that most therapists have between patients. If you are uncertain after this brief telephone discussion, make an appointment to meet the therapist face-to-face to learn more about her approach and to see if you are comfortable with her style, prior to making a final decision. Experienced therapists are very comfortable being interviewed in this way; after all, they are being asked to make a commitment to you, too. You should expect to pay the therapist's regular fee for this consultation; it will be worth it. If you connect with the therapist, you will have made a good start. If not, you will have saved yourself a great deal of time and money and perhaps some uncomfortable feelings as well.

Questions to Ask Potential Therapists

- **Are you licensed to practice in your field?**

I strongly advise against working with any professional who is not licensed, with the exception of advanced trainees or junior staff in reputable training centers who are working under the close supervision of senior, licensed professionals.

- **How long have you been in practice?**

There is no reason not to see a newly licensed psychologist or social worker or a child psychiatrist who has just completed her fellowship if she comes highly recommended by someone you trust. If you must find a therapist on your own, however, you may wish to choose someone with a few more years of experience.

- **Where did you do your internship, residency, fellowship?**

The answer to this question can provide helpful information about the extent of the professional's focus on working with children and families.

- **What is your approach?**

This can be a difficult question for a therapist to answer in a brief telephone call, but it is still a fair one and can tell you quite a bit about the person you are asking to advise you about some of the most important issues in your life. Do not be put off by a therapist who answers your question and then says that the best way to answer this would be to meet in person. I would think twice, however, about consulting a therapist who refused even to try to answer your question.

• **Are you a member of the national organization in your discipline?**

This is an important question, since national organizations develop and enforce adherence to codes of professional and ethical conduct. While membership in such organizations is not mandatory, it is usual. A professional who is not a member of her professional organization may have chosen not to join; she may also have been dropped from membership because of an ethical infraction.

• **Are you board certified?**

Board certification is the norm in both general and child psychiatry, and you should expect any competent and adequately trained child psychiatrist to be board certified in child and adolescent psychiatry; the same is true for general psychiatry.

In psychology, board certification means more when it is present than when it is absent. Knowing that a psychologist is board certified by the American Board of Professional Psychology means a great deal: the psychologist has chosen to have his work evaluated and scrutinized by a group of very senior psychologists and has obtained certification of superior proficiency. On the other hand, knowing that a psychologist is not board certified means very little since the majority of practicing psychologists, including some of the best, are not board certified. It would be a mistake to exclude a psychologist who has come highly recommended just because she is not boarded. Asking about this credential is most useful when you need to choose from among several psychologists without benefit of a personal recommendation.

• **What percentage of your practice is with children or families?** Unless you are seeking personal therapy for personal issues only and do not foresee any wish to talk about your children, your relationships with them, or their relationships with each other, look for someone who spends a significant part of her professional time with children and families, at least 50 percent.

Organizations Providing Referral Assistance

For Psychologists

American Psychological Association
    800-374-2723
    http://helping.apa.org/refer.html contains listings for all state psychological associations with addresses and telephone numbers.

National Register of Health Service Providers in Psychology
    202-783-7663
    http://www.nationalregister.com
    email natlregstr@aol.com

For Psychiatry

American Academy of Child and Adolescent Psychiatry
    800-333-7636
    http://www.aacap.org

For Social Workers

National Association of Social Workers
    800-638-8799
    http://www.socialworkers.org

SOME USEFUL BOOKS
FOR PARENTS

Your Baby and Child: From Birth to Age Five by Penelope Leach. New York: Knopf, 1997.

Siblings Without Rivalry: How to Help Your Children Live Together So You Can Too by Adele Faber and Elaine Mazlish. New York: Avon Books, 1998.

Understanding Your Child's Temperament by William B. Carey, M.D. New York: Macmillan, 1997.

Raising a Thinking Child: Help Your Young Child to Resolve Everyday Conflicts & Get Along with Others by Myrna B. Shure, Ph.D. New York: Pocket Books, 1996.

Sleeping Through the Night: How Infants, Toddlers and Their Parents Can Get a Good Night's Sleep by Jodi A. Mindell. New York: Harper Perennial, 1997.

Your One-Year-Old and other books in the Gesell Institute of Human Development Series (covering ages up to *Your Ten-to-Fourteen-Year-Old*) by Louise Bates Ames, Ph.D., and Frances L. Ilg, M.D. New York: Dell, various dates.

Books for Young Children

The Seven Silly Eaters by Mary Ann Hoberman and Marla Frazee. San Diego: Browndeer Press/Harcourt Brace, 1997.

The New Baby by Fred Rogers. New York: Paperstar/Penguin Putnam, 1995.

The New Baby at Your House by Joanna Cole, with photographs by Margaret Miller. New York: Morrow, 1985.

Arthur's Baby by Marc Brown. Boston: Little, Brown, 1987.

The Runaway Bunny by Margaret Wise Brown, illustrated by Clement Hurd. New York: Harper Collins, 1942. Not a sibling book, per se, but a must for any very young child's library. This picture book, by the author and illustrator of the classic *Goodnight Moon*, beautifully and gently speaks to children's delight in running away and being pursued by a loving parent.

INDEX

ABOUT THE AUTHOR

Peter Goldenthal, Ph.D., is a Board Certified Clinical and Family Psychologist and the author of two widely read family therapy textbooks. He received his training at Cornell University, the University of Connecticut, and Harvard Medical School. Dr. Goldenthal has held teaching positions at Bryn Mawr College, the University of Pennsylvania, the University of Delaware, and Jefferson Medical College and speaks frequently to groups of parents and professionals. Dr. Goldenthal practices in Wayne, Pennsylvania, and at the Children's Seashore House of Children's Hospital of Philadelphia where he directs the Child and Family Therapy Service and teaches advanced trainees in psychology and pediatrics. He lives near Philadelphia with his wife and two young children.

AUTHOR'S NOTE

I am very interested in hearing about your experiences using the concepts and strategies I have given you in *Beyond Sibling Rivalry*. If you have experiences you would like to share with me, or if you would like information about arranging a lecture or workshop, you may write to me in care of Henry Holt and Company at 115 West 18th Street, New York, NY 10011. If you prefer, you may send a fax directly to me at 610-687-4133, or an E-mail to Dr. Goldenthal@Family Resources.com.